transitions in the early years

Education at SAGE

SAGE is a leading international publisher of journals, books, and electronic media for academic, educational, and professional markets.

Our education publishing includes:

- accessible and comprehensive texts for aspiring education professionals and practitioners looking to further their careers through continuing professional development

- inspirational advice and guidance for the classroom

- authoritative state of the art reference from the leading authors in the field

Find out more at: **www.sagepub.co.uk/education**

transitions in the early years

working with children and families

edited by

lyn trodd

Los Angeles | London | New Delhi
Singapore | Washington DC

Los Angeles | London | New Delhi
Singapore | Washington DC

SAGE Publications Ltd
1 Oliver's Yard
55 City Road
London EC1Y 1SP

SAGE Publications Inc.
2455 Teller Road
Thousand Oaks, California 91320

SAGE Publications India Pvt Ltd
B 1/I 1 Mohan Cooperative Industrial Area
Mathura Road
New Delhi 110 044

SAGE Publications Asia-Pacific Pte Ltd
3 Church Street
#10-04 Samsung Hub
Singapore 049483

Editor: Jude Bowen
Assistant editor: Miriam Davey
Production editor: Nicola Marshall
Copyeditor: Neil Dowden
Proofreader: Mary Dalton
Indexer: Martin Hargreaves
Marketing manager: Lorna Patkai
Cover design: Wendy Scott
Typeset by: C&M Digitals (P) Ltd., Chennai, India
Printed by MPG Books Group, Bodmin, Cornwall

First published 2013

Library of Congress Control Number: 2012939336

British Library Cataloguing in Publication data

A catalogue record for this book is available from
the British Library

MIX
Paper from
responsible sources
FSC® C018575
www.fsc.org

ISBN 978-1-4462-4977-2
ISBN 978-1-4462-4978-9 (pbk)

Contents

About the editor and contributors

The editor

Dr Lyn Trodd is Head of Multi-Professional Education at the University of Hertfordshire. She is Chair of the National Network of Sector-Endorsed Foundation Degrees in Early Years. Lyn has published and edited a range of articles, national and international conference papers, and books focusing on the promotion of self-efficacy in children and practitioners, professional identity development and inter-professional working.

The contributors

David Allen is a Deputy Head of a junior school in Watford. He has worked in education for 18 years. During this time he has taught in Northamptonshire, Harrow, London, Hertfordshire and Spain. He has had several articles published in educational journals and is currently working on his first children's story book.

Julia Bateson is an education consultant with 27 years' experience teaching and leading in schools. She chairs a Children's Centre board and is a National Critical Friend. She is a director of an app game social enterprise empowering children to make digital media multicultural, health and well-being games for their peers.

Pamela Curran has extensive experience in community nursing and has spent the last eight years as a health visitor in Hertfordshire. She volunteers with children's groups to foster the welfare of young people and supports families through shared care. She trained in Bristol and spent some time working in Canada.

Mariana Graham is a qualified social worker who started working with neglected and abused children in South Africa. She continued to work with children and their families after she moved to the United Kingdom in November 2000. She has worked as a frontline social worker and manager and for the last six years as a Child Protection Conference Chair.

Dulcie Hiscott is a Children's Centre Coordinator. She worked previously as an outreach worker for two and a half years and in childcare for 15 years. She is now pursuing a career in children's centre management and working towards her master's degree.

Helen Longstaff is the manager of a Sure Start Children's Centre in a densely populated urban town with many social needs. She was a registered childminder for many years and then worked for the local authority to support and develop new and existing childcare.

Helena Marks is a Parent Partnership Adviser with experience in SEND, counselling, psychology and mental health who has worked in Hertfordshire for ten years. She is a recognised Early Support trainer for Hertfordshire in addition to delivering workshops to parents and practitioners and leading on an Early Years project.

Alison McLauchlin is a Senior Lecturer at the University of Hertfordshire. She is a fellow of the HEA and has worked as a consultant for Teachers TV. Alison previously taught in primary schools for 13 years, developing her expertise in special educational needs. She is also a parent of two adopted children.

Jennifer Lee McStravick is a Centre Manager who has worked in Hertfordshire for six years. Previously she led community arts fundraising, and community development for local councils. Before working in the Sure Start programme she had a strategic role supporting the development of extended schools in a London borough.

Lydia Ottavio is a Family Nurse (Family Nurse Partnership) and is studying Early Years at master's level. After training in Durham as a nurse and midwife, she practised midwifery for 18 years in the UK, Canada and the Middle East, then trained as a health visitor in Hertfordshire and worked in that role for 13 years.

Sally Patterson is a trained dramatherapist with experience of doing therapeutic work with families in a social service family centre. She has trained and supervised other professionals running community-based parenting programmes. She is currently manager of a Home-Start scheme, managing staff and volunteers to support families in their own homes.

Emma Perry is a qualified teacher who currently works for two Children's Centres, supporting the provision of good quality Early Years experiences for all children and their families. She has worked in Hertfordshire for eight years and is currently part way through her MA in Early Years at the University of Hertfordshire.

Amanda Ricciardi trained as a primary school teacher and has been a Pre-school Leader for five years. Her interest in Early Years education began as her own children attended pre-school and she chaired the committee of a setting. She is beginning to work towards Early Years Professional Status.

Anne Ross is a behavioural psychologist specialising in autism and ADHD. Since 1996 she has been involved in developing the voluntary and community organisation ADD-vance through her own family and personal experiences as well as her professional work. She currently manages a team of specialist ASD/ADHD coaches and family workers.

Preface

The idea for this book arose when Hertfordshire Local Authority commissioned the School of Education of the University of Hertfordshire to design and provide a master's-level course for senior practitioners supporting children's transitions. The intention was that participants would explore and research children's transitions in an interprofessional learning community and thus develop the strength and effectiveness of the 'Team around the Child' (Siraj-Blatchford et al., 2007) and, more recently, 'Think Family' and 'Team around the Family' strategy. In addition, the course would be a trial that may develop ideas for further courses across the country.

My colleague Leo Chivers and I were the lead tutors for the course although a range of other colleagues from across the university were involved. Leo and I were charged with devising its content and approach in collaboration with a steering group of service leaders from Hertfordshire. Our brief from our local authority colleague, David Shevlane, was to engage in a 'blue sky thinking' approach to the course. We should be innovative in creating new 'reflective spaces' (Jones and Gallop, 2003) for practitioners to have time to think together about how things could be better for children and families. The course would be externally evaluated on behalf of the then Department of Children, Schools and Families which was looking for new ways of bringing services together to support children's transitions and improve their life chances.

One of the features which we developed was that course participants would use two different research approaches in their assessed work:

critical or significant incident analysis (Brookfield, 1990) in which participants would identify a significant event relating to a child's transition and reflect critically and systematically on its meaning and significance; and Appreciative Inquiry (Cooperider et al., 2003) in which they would explore change by focusing on what works rather than what fails, strengths rather than weaknesses and possibilities rather than problems. Another feature was to build in time for participants to visit each other's work contexts and to explain their practice to each other in learning groups. In order to develop reflection and self-awareness we used experiential methods in the taught sessions based on group enquiry activities. However, probably the most powerful 'innovation' was simply to gather all of the professionals together and to facilitate the time, space and stimulus for them to share, debate and explore their work with children and families experiencing transitions.

Twenty-seven professionals from a range of children's services enrolled on the programme. Together we co-constructed the course. Each participant and tutor engaged with its challenges with enthusiasm, good humour and a proactive approach to the inevitable uncertainty experienced. The chapters that follow are written mainly by some of these same course participants and are constructed from their practitioner research. The book also includes two further chapters written by authors with particular insight into children's transitions, one from a parental perspective and the other from a deputy head teacher. We wanted to write the kind of book that we would have liked to have had available to us when we came together on the course or when we were new in post. A student group can use one of the case studies as set reading and then focus on the dilemmas that follow it as group discussion points or, alternatively, the case study can be used as material for a 'hot seat' activity in which a student role plays the family member, the child or the practitioner and is questioned by the rest of the class.

One of the aims of the book is to explore a wider definition of the notion of transition applied to very young children and their families and to include examples of how family transitions impact on the lives of children and how professional transitions shape the services designed to support children and their families. Each chapter tells one or more stories in the form of case studies of transitions giving a rich picture of professional responsibility and accountability in the complexities of decision-making. The chapters are written from the perspectives of a wide range of professionals working with children and

families although there is no claim that every single one is repre-
sented. They offer the reader a chance to view transitions through an
authentic and interprofessional lens and to share in some moments
of job satisfaction as well as dilemmas and frustrations.

The book depicts some of the realities of working to support children's
transitions. In order to be able to portray feelings and events openly
the case study stories are constructed from a synthesis of each author's
extensive experience. Any names or incidents described do not repre-
sent a real person or incident unless specific permission from the client was secured. We hope you recognise aspects of your own personal
and professional experiences in at least one chapter and are able to
identify with the author or the case study. However, if you read the
other chapters you will have an opportunity to understand better
both the experiences of children and their families in transition and
the work of colleagues from other professions who are working as
your fellow members of teams around children and their families.

Acknowledgements

Thank you to Hertfordshire's Childhood Support Services for entrusting the School of Education with the leadership of such an exciting project.

I am very grateful to the contributors for their resilience and honesty in writing their chapters and to their families and employers for allowing them the time and space to write.

It is important to express warm thanks to my University of Hertfordshire colleague, Leo Chivers, with whom it was fun and interesting to collaborate on the course and then to begin to conceptualise this book.

Jude Bowen from Sage and her team have been immensely supportive and patient.

Lastly, thank you to my family for their love, support and encouragement. If only everyone had such a team around them.

Lyn Trodd

For my students, past and present, from whom I have learned so much.

Introduction

Lyn Trodd

Children and transitions

Our awareness of the importance of paying attention to children's transitions is a modern phenomenon. When children were evacuated to the country from London and other major cities during the Second World War, some of the advice to parents was to pretend to children that they were going on holiday or even to refrain from discussing what was about to occur. The received wisdom was that children would be better off not knowing what was happening than being fussed or worried about it. Consequently, there was little or no preparation of most of the children being evacuated or any account taken of the way the evacuees would experience such a huge change in their lives and its potential impact on their future well-being. Similarly, when their mothers were about to have a new baby or their parent was to remarry, it was common to send children to stay with family members or neighbours to get them out of the way. Then, after the event, the children were presented with any changes to the family structure as a 'fait accompli'. Children's rights to know about and have a say in what was happening to them were not considered to be of significance. Adults did not hold it important or appropriate to promote children's agency and autonomy in matters to do with their own lives. In fact, in general, the aim was for children to be as dutiful and compliant as possible.

Several decades later, society officially recognises that children have rights. Article 12 of the United Nations Convention on the Rights of the Child (1989) requires that every child has the right to a voice on matters that affect them and to have their views taken seriously – in accordance with their age and maturity. Since 1997 there has been increasing political interest in smoothing transitions (Ecclestone in Field et al., 2009). It seems linked to a desire to encourage social inclusion and participation and a drive to minimise disadvantage. There is awareness that children's well-being and development can be influenced by the manner in which they experience transitions: 'transitions are stressful for children and young people, just as they are for adults, and the resulting stress can have far-reaching effects on children's emotional well-being and academic achievements' (www.youngminds.org.uk/training_services/young_minds_in_schools/wellbeing/transitions (accessed 20 October 2012)). As a result of political and professional concerns 'supporting transitions' became one aspect of the Common Core of Skills and Knowledge: 'it is important to understand a child ... in the context of their life, to recognise and understand the impact of any transitions they may be going through' (CWDC, 2010: 16).

Although it is identified as one of six key areas of expertise and skills for everyone working with children, those developing training and education for those who work with children were initially reluctant to acknowledge it. Six months after the publication of the Common Core, Johnson et al. reported that relatively little attention was being paid to 'Supporting Transitions' in training and education for work with children. When compared to the five other areas of expertise and skills required for members of the Children's Workforce, 'data highlights the relatively low coverage in modules of the area' (Johnson et al., 2005: 7).

The revised standards for Early Years Professional Status include: 1.4 Support children through a range of transitions (Teaching Agency, 2012: 15). Some social services have developed the role of Transitions Worker (Leeds Multi-agency Transition Strategy 2010–2015, 2012) and the Department for Education is promoting a National Transition Support Team and a National Transitions Programme for all local authorities (www.education.gov.uk/childrenandyoungpeople/sen/ahdc/a0067510/local-transition-support (accessed 13 April 2012)).

Examination of the materials available and the standards and curricula in training shows that there is no consistency in the way that transitions are conceptualised. This matters because it is likely to create difficulties when agencies and services try to work together to support children and their families. It is important to pay attention to the constructs of transitions held by adults, such as parents and practitioners working with children because they influence their relationships with children and each other. What they think constitutes a 'good' transition and how they think appropriate support can be given is drawn from their views and, in turn, influences children's experiences of transitions. Some of the views are formed from individuals' own experiences. Some are influenced by the professional values and practices and personal perspectives of individuals. In the chapters that follow some of those values, practices and perspectives will be visible.

In a review of research into transitions Vogler et al. (2008) characterise transitions as:

- socio-cultural stages marked by community understanding and representation of lives (rites of passage);

- institutional stages often led by biological readiness;

- horizontal movements between the different daily contexts inhabited by children;

- historical and global changes that impact on a child's life;

- choices made for and by children.

However, in practice, most inquiries into children's experiences of transitions tend to focus on structural changes such as moving from one Key Stage to another or into new settings. The outcomes are used to generate guidance and advice for parents and practitioners in order that they may support children more effectively through and after moves. The ultimate aim is to make the process of transition as smooth and continuous as possible. Transitions are conceptualised as 'risky shifts' in which children may need practical and emotional support and help. Some strategies aim to ensure that children will experience the most seamless change possible, so that new learning builds on previous knowledge without regression in performance levels or loss of momentum in learning. Some are principled approaches driven by recognition of children's rights. Some are motivated by understanding that transitions in the Early Years that are poorly supported are likely to diminish children's future resilience in times of change.

Seeing transitions as only problematic is problematic in itself. It is a view that contrasts sharply with a traditional view of transitions as rites of passage that occur to mark changes in both family and social status. Rites of passage for children and young people are generally characterised as positive strides forward and as inevitable and anticipated progressions in life that are marked by social rituals or celebrations. They are often occasions on which society recognises that the child is maturing and gaining agency, rights and responsibilities. In western cultures there tend to be only a few transitions in our lives that are given cultural recognition, for instance bar or bat mitzvahs, weddings, funerals and graduations. In fact, adults and children go through many transitions that are not marked by society.

A thought-provoking way to explore children's experiences of transitions is to consider them in relation to Bandura's theory of self-efficacy which he defines as 'people's beliefs about their capabilities to produce designated levels of performance that exercise influence over events that affect their lives' (1986: 391). He argues that efficacy beliefs are the foundation of human agency. 'Unless people believe they can produce desired results and forestall detrimental ones by their actions, they have little incentive to act or to persevere in the face of difficulties' (Bandura, 2001: 11). According to Bandura (1994: 3), an individual can be exposed to four sources of information about their own self-efficacy. They relate to: (1) 'mastery experiences' or experiences of success; (2) seeing people similar to oneself manage task demands successfully; (3) social persuasion that one has the capabilities to succeed in given activities; and (4) inferences from somatic (physical) and emotional states indicative of personal strengths and vulnerabilities.

When Bandura's theory is used to explore children's experiences of transitions we begin to see how adults can support children better if they understand that:

1 a mastery experience of successful transition promotes resilience and self-efficacy in the face of a later transition but conversely a negative experience may deplete them;

2 observing positive transitions of others with whom children identify helps them to see their own transitions as normal and unthreatening;

3 emotional and social support and the opportunity to absorb stories of transitions can increase a child's belief in his or her own capacity to navigate a transition successfully;

4 self-awareness, acquisition of a related vocabulary and concepts that enable the child to understand the transition as well as general well-being may diminish feelings of anxiety and vulnerability

In fact, in lived experiences, transitions are layered, messy and complex. They might be 'risky shifts' and anticipated rites of passage at the same time; for example, a child starting 'big school' may love having a new school uniform and the present from granddad and granny to open on arriving home that marks a rite of passage to becoming a school pupil. However, the same child might be too anxious about going to school to eat breakfast for several weeks whilst his or her expectations of self and life become recalibrated. Ecclestone et al. (2005) suggest that we need to see transitions as both events such as turning points and life stage signifiers but also more subtle processes of personal adjustment and identity development through subjective self-conceptualisation in role, context or in a situation.

Part of the identity development resulting from transitions derives from the stories that people hear and tell themselves and others about what is happening to them, who they are and what they can do. A story is constructed and told by an 'author' as an intentional communication. It usually involves some sort of transformative moment and is told as a sequence of events within a defined time period. Stories are everywhere: 'We dream in narrative, daydream in narrative, remember, anticipate, hope, despair, plan, revise, criticize, gossip, learn, hate and love by narrative' (Hardy, 1968: 5). A story or 'a personal narrative' (Quinn Patton, 2002: 116) is a construct as well as a means for the teller to communicate their version of reality. The teller does not just empty out his or her thoughts but crafts and organises the story purposefully. When children and their families are telling stories of their experience of a transition they are establishing their version of events to themselves and the listener or reader. Much can be learned from paying close attention to their perspectives. Whilst the contributors relate their stories of transitions in the case studies and reflections, they are also narrating their practice and professional identities. The reader who wishes to develop interprofessionally has an opportunity to see how each contributor sees their practice and role.

Formal and informal narratives that accompany recognised transitions function as a means of teaching children to cope through anticipatory planning. Sometimes they learn to look forward to the transition with pleasure and excitement. The narratives or 'stories' that portray transitions are powerful influences on a child's experience of a transition.

Social stories (Briody and McGarry, 2005) can rehearse the experience before it happens and often fill in the gaps that adults forget to explain because they take children's knowledge and understanding for granted. They provide information about what will happen and when it will happen in the manner of visual scripts. They can empower children by giving them language and concepts with which to take control of their own stories of transitions and organise and interpret events.

In the chapters that follow the reader may notice key moments when children or family members in a case study begin to find a voice and take charge of their story and thus they are heard in relation to the transitions being experienced. Often being in charge of the story or not to some degree is what defines a good or bad transition in the view of the case study children and their families. Some of the chapters focus on how the 'voice of the child' can be heard even when that appears to be very difficult. There are suggestions that the child's views can be accessed through parents or practitioners who work with the child on a daily basis.

One issue that rightly troubles practitioners working to support children and families is how far belief that professional support for transitions is necessary assumes that they are helpless and vulnerable and unable to navigate their own way through the change facing them. In addition, a 'deficit' approach to children and families may disregard the learning and personal growth that can be achieved through dealing successfully with transitions without the help of social agencies. It is important to look for promise and potential not just problems and deficits. Transitions can be viewed and experienced as opportunities to learn and change rather than potentially risky, depleting events (Page, 2000). There is a boundary between facilitating an entitlement to support for a transition and actively intervening in another's life in a way that reduces his or her agency. The authors of the chapters portray this aspect of their work as a complex professional 'dance' in which they have to be ready to move forward and backward with equal sensitivity and agility.

Kübler-Ross's grief model (1969) is often used to explain the experience of a transition in terms of loss. The five stages of reactions to a death described by Kübler-Ross (denial, anger, bargaining, depression and acceptance) are used to understand potential reactions to far less traumatic changes than the death of a friend or family member. The model aligns comfortably with a Piagetian notion of learning, i.e. transitions create dissonance which leads to disequilibration and eventually it leads to accommodation. However, because it was first described in relation to bereavement, it depicts transitions in pathological terms, i.e. change is painful and difficult, rather than as a normal part of life.

What can make a transition difficult is when it is sudden and unexpected and the child or family member does not have time to adjust. Anticipated, gradual transitions are easier to deal with. Children find transitions that involve changes to relationships with people they are close to and dependent upon the most uncomfortable. They can appear sad, lethargic and find it difficult to engage with new things and to learn. Other factors that exacerbate transitions are when a number of transitions occur at the same time or close together such as family break-up, a house move or new sibling. In addition it can be more difficult for children to cope when they are vulnerable because of other circumstances such as illness or when a child is particularly young, has sensory impairment, English as an additional language or has special educational needs and disabilities.

According to Dowling (1995) the stakes are high as early experiences of transitions can affect learning and behaviour for life. Children will cope best if they are informed and consulted about changes, have a strong sense of identity and belonging and have general social and emotional well-being, resilience and good health. Emotional health and well-being and self-efficacy influence each other. Both strengths predispose people to being more resilient during and after unexpected transitions. Bird and Gerlach define emotional health and well-being in terms of self-efficacy beliefs as:

> the subjective capacity and state of mind that supports us to feel good about how we are and confident to deal with present and *future* circumstances [my emphasis]. It is influenced by our emotional development and how resilient and resourceful we feel ourselves to be. (Bird and Gerlach, 2005 in Roberts, 2006: 6)

For Bird and Gerlach (2005) a sense of identity, self-worth and a belief in their own ability to influence things and make changes are associated with a capacity to tolerate uncertainty. This provides a position of strength from which individuals can be resilient, respond positively to transitions as one of life's challenges and transfer any learning they acquire into the future.

However, adults can help to mitigate the impact of transitions especially on children's learning and development. Fabian (2002) advises that what sees children through a transition is if the support offered by parents and practitioners prevents a lack of continuity becoming significant and confusing. It is not easy for adults to know when they need to intervene and what their responsibilities are in a child's transitions. They have a delicate balance to observe between supporting children's transition and lessening their agency in their own lives by assuming that children are not capable and not resilient.

There are some principles that adults can adhere to confidently. They should listen carefully to children, including the use of observations and sources of information from parents and practitioners who interact with children on a daily basis. They must be alert to signs of troubled transitions and record and report their concerns. They need to maintain confidentiality and be respectful of the child's sense of self and emotional well-being. Importantly they need to work to create links and partnerships between the interconnected micro and macro systems that are the child's world so that he or she is enabled to feel suitable (Broström, 2002), secure, recognised and able to participate (Woodhead and Brooker, 2008), and be 'like fish in water' (Laevers et al., 1997: 15) with a sense of belonging.

A key factor in creating links and partnerships for successful transitions is the quality of relationships between children, their families, friends and peers and the practitioners and professionals. For Pianta et al. (1995) transitions are a 'process of relationship formation' (cited in Brooker, 2008: 151). Brooker (2008) argues that when relationships are the most challenging and fraught to initiate and maintain, they are probably the most important relationships that are needed for successful transitions. There is a need to achieve a balance of power and mutual respect in relationships between the adults around the child. Someone has to take responsibility for reaching out to make the first contact. It is important to be sensitive to misunderstandings which may lead to individuals feeling that their voices are not heard or valued.

A significant aspect of the promotion of good relationships between adults involved with the child to ensure successful transitions is a commitment to interprofessionalism. Transitions require the highest level of interprofessional working. In the chapters that follow there are numerous examples of the challenges of working interprofessionally to create the threads of the safety net for transitions. Whilst social policies and children's rights legislation demand that practitioners centre on the needs of each individual child, in fact they are working in a context in which they have to have multiple priorities and work with others who have competing powers over the work that they do.

The child is likely to be just one of the priorities in family settings and community services. This theme is explored in some of the chapters.

In addition, children are understood to be 'nested' in micro and macro systems that include their family and friends and social agencies (Bronfenbrenner, 1986) and so must not be viewed in isolation but in relation to these contexts. As a result practitioners are more aware that transitions experienced by family members are as likely to impact on children as their own transitions might. They are conscious that professional transitions may influence the quality of the support offered to children and families. In recognition of this reality some of the chapters focus on the 'situatedness' of children's experience of transitions, exploring its interplay with professional interactions with families in which there are young children.

Given the recognition in this chapter to the range of constructs of transitions that exist and practitioners' multiple perspectives on what they are, it is not easy to devise a working definition of 'transition' for this book. At a very simple level transition is an experience of change. A unifying assumption between the chapter authors is that a transition is more than an event. It is a process that is experienced and has a meaning to transitioning individuals that is likely to shape their lives as they continue on moving between two states of being, i.e. becoming different.

Birth

Lydia Ottavio

Chapter Overview

This chapter aims to develop your understanding of aspects of birth as a transition. Practitioners working with young children draw on their professional experience and training and also from their own experiences as a sibling to understand the experience of birth as a transition. They know that the birth of a new member of the family can create not only delight but also insecurity and troubled behaviour in siblings, particularly those who are close in age to the new-born family member. New parents may experience a change in identity, lifestyle and family relationships. In this chapter a health visitor argues that birth is a transition experienced by the whole family. This can compound its impact on young children, and when we view it in this way we are better able to support children and families as an interprofessional team. Birth may be a ubiquitous experience in life and a common occurrence in society, but there is no doubt it feels like a unique experience for the individuals in the family. As a health visitor, it is a privilege to be involved in this major life transition from pregnancy, to birth and after. However, the best support for a family relies on leadership skills that reach across agencies to link up with other professionals so that the most responsive and sensitive services are mobilised.

Introduction to the case study

The antenatal period is a very important and undervalued transition. Transition to parenthood affects the unborn baby as well as the whole family, and pregnancy and the first years of life are crucial to development; the seeds are planted for future health and well-being. If this period is disrupted, if parents fail to bond with their child, emotional problems could result and babies become at risk of disadvantage and impaired development.

The chapter presents a case study of a birth in a family. It is presented from the perspective of the baby before and after birth. First, there is an example of some problems met by a family in which a new baby is soon to be born. Then, things improve largely because of good 'interventions' by the health visitor. Next, the health visitor reflects on the case study explaining what was happening in order to illuminate understanding of the transition process. Finally, the health visitor discusses aspects of her own role and leadership skills while working with other professionals and agencies to support the child and family through this major life transition. The chapter closes with some thoughts from the health visitor on what she has learned from the case and how she and her team will seek to change their approach.

 Soon to be born ... baby Luca

I'm waiting to be born and be part of the outside world. My parents are Anglo-Italian; living with us are aunties, grandparents, cousins; and it's noisy. Mummy is quiet; she helps look after my poorly Nan while Auntie makes pesto and pasta. Daddy works hard in a city; I hear his voice at weekends. Auntie worries about Mummy, not caring for herself – bad eating, late rising, no energy and missing her midwife appointments. Despite this I'm doing well. It helps Mummy doesn't smoke or drink alcohol.

Oh – some movement – Auntie seems to be taking Mummy somewhere in her pyjamas. Is it to hospital or the surgery? They are both annoyed with the midwife, will they go again?

Back at home, more problems for Auntie. My cousin can't go back to nursery as he's not potty trained. He is very lively around the house. Cross voices.

A new midwife visits, with a health visitor. Mummy likes this one. There's lots of tears and Mummy says there is no-one to help. The midwife promises to help Mummy. A phone rings and she is called away. Maybe she is too busy?

Oh dear. Nan's doctor is here. Everyone's sad. Mummy is quiet, not eating Auntie's pasta. Where are the midwife and the health visitor? Who cares about Mummy and me?

I'm born! There's shouting about which creams to put on my rash. Nan scolds Mummy – she's crying but she won't have help from anyone. When I cry she doesn't hear me. When she holds me she stares into space. Here's the doctor to visit Nan. Will he notice how Mummy is?

My cousin tries to climb in my cot to be a baby with me. He is in trouble again. Mummy shouts at Auntie to keep him away ...

Things improve for baby Luca

I'm home and 12 days old. It's cosy with Mummy and Daddy, aunties, nanny and granddad, especially my cheeky cousin. Everyone's helping and Mummy's happier; I hear her voice more now. The health visitor and mid-wife give her ideas for baby groups to join; I'm looking forward to that.

At the group Mummy finds tips – childhood ailments, illnesses, safety and development. We learn about children's centres and baby-friendly places to go, and the librarian tells us about 'rhyme time' and 'story time' at the library.

My cousin is allowed to cuddle me – with help and supervision. Wow, he is lively and exciting! He can do so much – I love him. He makes Mummy laugh too. Mummy reads him a story about new babies and shows him how to play with me gently.

Mummy is talking, reading and singing to me more and more each day; great for my development and helps with bonding, social, emotional skills, and speech. I meet up with other babies, play on my tummy and enjoy the music Mummy plays for me. Life is good!

Mummy sees the doctor now who is very helpful, caring and interested in us. The midwife comes back. She is very kind. I feel safe, secure and happy now. All these professionals are aware of our family. There is so much help available for us.

This week I will be four months old! I have just come back from a spe-cial cinema with Mummy and Daddy, and lots of other families. They can change and feed me there and don't have to worry if I cry or make noises.

Great!

Dilemmas for the health visitor

There are four transition dilemmas highlighted in this case study. The first is how best to provide early support for the family, a shift of focus from postnatal support to more help in pregnancy (Sinclair, 2007). The second relates to how to develop better communication and information sharing whilst recognising that, as Leadbetter (2006) writes, new ways of working can cause difficult tensions in professional teams and across multi-professional services. The third is lack of team cohesion; having separate roles, responsibilities, working independently in our own spaces (Rushmer and Pallis, 2002). Finally, the fourth is how to give culturally sensitive information and advice, without making assumptions about another's beliefs. One person's mother–infant reactions can be very different from another's (Lynch and Hanson, 1992). This is particularly challenging when there are cultural and language differences between members of the family and the health visitor.

Early support for the family

The health visitor in the case study was part of an 'Early Support' project, a new venture for local midwives, GPs, health visitors and a wider team of professionals. They meet weekly at a children's centre to discuss referrals face to face (Regan and Ireland, 2009). Quarterly 'formal' meetings include the wider team and managers. Letters to GPs explain the project, posters and flyers are distributed, and they obtain consent from clients to work using this different approach. However, they are worried that transition and relationship issues that they came across are being referred too late to support vulnerable families. Naturally the top priority is to save the lives of babies or mothers. Lower down the agenda are family and social relationships. The challenge remains to energise their team to think broadly and creatively about when early support may benefit families (Davies and Brighouse, 2010) and prevent difficulties developing.

A positive antenatal period is vital for baby's brain development. If the potential for a special relationship between professionals and the family can be developed, much can be achieved. There can be positive outcomes for bonding, breast feeding, child health and development (Larson, 1980). Postnatal depression and accidents can be reduced if supportive networks are enhanced (DOH, 2009a).

Communication and information sharing

Communication, confidentiality and information sharing among professionals are crucial to effective support for the family – which needs to be seen as a holistic unit as well as composed of individuals. Historically, lack of 'sharing' information by health visitors and midwives has meant a gap in service provision. When we share skills, we learn so much more (Ancona et al., 2007). Joint working offers opportunities for discussion, openness and fluid information and skill-sharing that can lead to more responsive services. However, trust takes time to develop between professionals. One way to build interprofessional trust is to work and train together including 'shadowing' each other to appreciate our roles (Mintzberg, 1998).

CAF (Common Assessment Framework) training across professional boundaries develops understanding, encourages responsible risk-taking and learning from new experiences, and builds strong associations with colleagues (Leadbetter, 2006). Holding joint meetings in neutral venues such as the children's centre means we can all 'own' the space and develop mutual understanding of responsibilities (HM Government, 2010). Interprofessional team-working helps sense-making, relating, visioning and inventing but it also provides live links that create a safety net for children and their families.

It is really helpful when professionals ensure that there are opportunities to update each other on new developments; for instance a health visitor can organise her team to receive updates from midwives on issues like breast feeding. Actions like this improve professional relationships and understanding and can be surprisingly well received. Crucially, provision of timely and relevant information to families can 'head off' difficulties. As the auntie in this case study said: 'The health visitor has been a tower of strength, giving us information on a number of our concerns.'

Team cohesion

In this case study the family did not receive connected care from the midwife, health visitor, doctor and other professionals from the start (Regan and Ireland, 2009). Perhaps lack of team cohesion – having separate roles and responsibilities, working independently in their own centres (Rushmer and Pallis, 2002) – limited the responsiveness of care services to the needs of the child and the family. A co-ordinated team approach, in partnership with parents, can address a host of difficulties such as depression, accident prevention, nutrition and dental care (Hall and Elliman, 2003). Meeting in the family home can help to identify a broad range of medical and family needs. In this case the GP knew of the grandmother's illness, but not the client's pregnancy and opportunities were lost to consider the impact of one aspect of the family's circumstances on another.

Hosking and Walsh (2005) emphasise that if there is sensitive care and good attachment to key people such as parents in the early years, children will grow up appreciating others' feelings, being able to empathise and be secure and resilient. However, the road to parenting is difficult, isolating and frightening (Cowan and Cowan, 2000). Marriage/relationship difficulties may affect parenting which, in turn, is likely to affect the child's overall development. The challenging outcomes to work for are children who are less violent, better behaved and with fewer mental health problems as they grow up.

Early referrals and interventions may prevent difficulties, and ease relationship building (Field, 2010). An example of positive joined-up working is when a CAF assessment of a pregnant teenage pupil sets up a meeting at her school, so professionals from health, education and the children's centre can adopt a team approach that creates seamless support for her and around her. The focus must be working 'with' the client, keeping their needs as the central concern (DoH, 2000).

Cultural sensitivity

Awareness that the person working with a child and their family is giving 'culturally sensitive' information and support is important. With the best will in the world the intervention intended to support the child and family may be unfamiliar or families may be vulnerable during a difficult transition. In addition, professional 'help' can be overpowering (Lynch and Hanson, 1992). Illich (2000: 17) states this point clearly: 'they not only recommend what is good, but actually ordain what is right'. Families may feel pressured to do what 'professionals want' instead of being empowered to do what they desire once given the facts and advice. Professionals are good at 'giving' advice, instead of finding out what people want. Illich (2000) challenges us about 'knowing best'. Being culturally aware requires flexibility, an open heart, and a willingness to accept different perspectives using a sensitive and respectful approach and taking unobtrusive actions (Mintzberg, 1998).

In the case study the health visitor suggested baby groups, baby massage and seeing a mental health worker, but any one of these hold the potential to upset the family's beliefs (Lynch and Hanson, 1992). The advice on 'research-based' creams was not well received. The family agreed out of politeness and continued their own practice after the health visitor left. She talked about 'potty training' as an intentional practice, assuming the family understood. However, it was not in the family's vocabulary. For this family, the child gains control of her bowels through a natural progression from birth which follows the baby's cues and mother's reactions (Lynch and Hanson, 1992). When reflecting in her professional log, this health visitor recollected that, when she was in Africa with the Masai, breastfeeding mothers knew when their babies were going to 'perform' and never used nappies.

Keeping a professional log like this highlights the benefits of writing experiences down, thinking about what happened, and forming fresh views after 'chewing it over' (Bolton, 2001). The health visitor was mindful of 'border crossing' (Moss, 2008) or collaborating with others to become aware of alternatives, learn from colleagues' expertise and experience, and be open to and curious about other ways of living and disciplines. So she talked things through with some colleagues. In this case study the health visitor's discussions with colleagues, such as the community psychiatric nurse, helped to identify solutions to some of the difficulties faced by the mum. She agreed with Ancona et al. (2007: 94) in her professional log: 'I appreciate a good leader is incomplete; having strengths, weaknesses but able to draw on others for skills they don't have'. Laming (2009) argues for organised, regular, reflective supervision and peer support to ensure sufficient effective support is available to the professionals who are supporting families.

Services should provide culturally sensitive, relevant information. Developing relationships with parents, social support and using effective leaflets are essential for health promotion (McKellar et al., 2009). It is the time spent listening to people's stories and the processes used to engage with families that make an important difference to the quality of care and support they receive. Tritschler and Yarwood (2007) recommends knowing ourselves as helpful to gaining insight into a family's needs, arguing that we can relate to the family using personal experience and knowledge. This is an ongoing process. We always have more learning to do.

A health visitor's perspective

Pregnancy and the first years of life are vital to development; seeds are planted for future health and well-being. As a health visitor (and previously a midwife), I believe this is a crucial and undervalued transition. Gerhardt discusses the 'toxicity of stress' on a vulnerable, developing baby. The baby's brain development is rapid during the months before birth and up to the age of five and if this process is disrupted babies may become disadvantaged with emotional and development problems (Gerhardt, 2004). As Sinclair (2007: 18) says: 'The most important six years in a person's life are up to the age of five.' Early intervention can improve the attachment process (Heywood, 2009). By identifying needs, giving support, we improve family outcomes, the child's well-being, and social and emotional development (Hosking and Walsh, 2005; DoH, 2009b).

Transition to parenthood is one of the most challenging periods of anyone's life (Cowan and Cowan, 2000; Berlin et al., 2005). With policy changes, lack of funding and modifications to the health visitor's role, families may only receive one home postnatal visit. This is a huge contrast to Scandinavia where the early postnatal period is considered precious (Sinclair, 2007) and much greater resources are devoted to supporting it.

In the case study, antenatal tension was seen. It is best that the health visitor endeavours to give positive, reassuring comments during visits at this time because occasionally families may be experiencing unhappiness and isolation rather than the joyful anticipation they expected. Later in the case study the newly qualified midwife engaged well with the family, was interested and they felt supported (Molyneux, 2001). Professional input through home visiting can improve parents' attitude and quality of the home environment (Kendrick et al., 2000). It can also help the health visitor to form an early picture of the family and establish a sound relationship.

The health visitor wrote in her professional log: 'In some ways we had failed this family. I met them very late on in the pregnancy, and it made it more difficult to form a trusting relationship.' Only one antenatal visit occurred, so opportunities to build confidence and trust were missed. Fortunately, relationships improved during the postnatal visits and the family fed back they were extremely grateful for her visits. The health visitor noted in her professional log that she was surprised how worried the mum was. The mum had said,

'The thought of meeting you [the health visitor] was quite scary'. The comment gave the health visitor pause for thought and caused her to consider ways to make the first meeting less threatening.

Many professionals were involved with this family which was surprising and confusing for all. Initially each health professional worked 'blindly'. However, sharing information is essential to ensure families get the support they require and may request. It entails honesty, openness and following up on plans, while keeping the child as the central focus. Pooling information while respecting confidentiality and gaining consent from clients enables liaison with a wider team which provides a holistic picture of the family that helps to improve and progress care (HM Government, 2010). The midwife knew the mother's dilemma; the GP had significant information about the grandparents' health needs; and the nursery nurse and health visitor saw multiple needs impacting on the unborn baby, parents, siblings and grandparents but the information was not shared effectively. Professionals undoubtedly felt they were giving the 'best' care. However, if they had taken a team approach, it would have helped to understand the family dynamics and may have improved support for everyone, even the health visitor herself. The health visitor wrote in her professional log: 'I felt a huge burden lay with me.' This is typical as ultimate responsibility often rests on the health visitor (Morrow et al., 2005).

In fact this family had many significant strong features. The mother and child had exceptionally good household support, rarely seen in British families as relatives often live hundreds of miles away (Lynch and Hanson, 1992). This family's situation improved after their needs were recognised and professionals were invited to work together (Foley and Rixon, 2008; Laming, 2009). The midwife saw that the mum appeared depressed in the antenatal period. She feared bonding between mother and baby would be affected (Cleaver et al., 2010). The mum consented to see her doctor in the postnatal period and gradually matters improved and strong bonds developed between mum and her baby. There was facial contact, cuddles and cooing and the mum became attuned to her baby.

Reflections

Because the health visitor's team was thoughtful, reflective and dedicated to doing their best for clients at all times, they drew up an action plan with recommendations to improve their leadership and support for the transitions of children and families. The health visitor recommended some changes in the way the team worked with families based on her learning and observations from this case study. This led to four priorities for action.

First, having observed that relationships between the health visitor and parents are affected by the timing and context of the initial encounter, the team agreed to be flexible about the time and place of the first meeting and to take note of the family's preferences. They brought forward the target date for meeting the parents-to-be and devised a 'criteria for referral' pack to formalise the record of early referrals as well as to act as an aide-mémoire.

Second, the team discussed how to improve information sharing and provide a seamless service for clients. They decided that to provide care without knowing what professionals from other services are doing is not a connected service. Their view was that joint working builds trust and develops understanding, making our expertise explicit, instead of tacit, for all professionals. Strong team cohesion gives families continuous seamless support that reaps rewards when things for the family are not going well. Early identification and consistent provision are crucial to protect our children (Leadbetter, 2006). One action was to take the time to give some positive feedback to other professionals when they had done a good job and a positive outcome for the family was achieved. This appeared to energise the wider team.

Third, in order to build team cohesion some joint training was arranged. The health visitor arranged for 'Bookstart' to give a training session in order to give colleagues from a range of professional backgrounds an insight into why books affect both bonding and socialisation. She wrote in her professional log: 'I think the leadership model "asilo per uccelli" (Italian for a "nest for birds") is a metaphor for nurturing and developing our teams so we can nurture and develop our children and families.'

Fourth, the health visitor realised that she and the team would benefit by being more culturally sensitive and self-aware, to avoid making assumptions regarding language and customs. For instance, one simple initiative was to find out more about what is available to families whose oral English is still developing. In the case study the interpreting services were brought in for important meetings to make sure that all members of the family could be included.

Stop Press! Update on the case study

All is well with the family. Mum and baby have an attuned, responsive relationship that bodes well for the future social integration, well-being and language development of the baby. Because of the successful outcome of this case the health visitor and her team felt encouraged and re-energised in their roles. They knew that early antenatal input would be paramount in improving this transition for families like this as well as giving babies the best start and outcomes in their lives and those around them (Olds et al., 2010). Our county has now commissioned the Family Nurse Partnership which offers the intensive early support for young first-time mothers. Family nurses (some may have health visiting, and/or midwifery experience) have begun this valuable, cost-effective work supporting families from early pregnancy; improving life chances of babies and future generations.

Further Reading

Gerhardt, S. (2011) *Why Love Matters: How Affection Shapes a Baby's Brain*. New York: Brunner-Routledge.

This book argues that early relationships are vital to create optimal well-being for future generations. It challenges some established views of what babies need, drawing on brain science to justify its arguments.

Murray, L. and Andrews, L. (2005) *The Social Baby*. Richmond: CP Publishing.

This book helps adults understand the communication of babies and how they can provide sensitive care. It includes photos of babies that give clues needed to begin to read and understand baby cues right from birth.

Rosengren, D. (2009) *Building Motivational Interviewing Skills*. London: Guilford Press.

This book is a great tool to use for positive behaviour change with clients and professionals, encouraging use of alternative wording to elicit behaviour changes in clients and in transition workers' professional and personal lives.

2

Home–pre-school–childminder–playgroup–home

Emma Perry

Chapter Overview

This chapter focuses on children in Early Years settings who experience multiple transitions in one day, i.e. children who move into different places during a fairly ordinary day. This area of transition is of particular interest to professionals working in children's centres which may offer a variety of provision for young children. The chapter takes the work of a qualified teacher (QT) as its professional focus. QTs may be working alongside other children's centres in their district. They are likely to seek ongoing working relationships with teachers, childminders, children's centre managers, Early Years consultants and Early Years practitioners in order to create the smoothest possible transition for children and their families as they move between settings. As Dunlop and Fabian state: 'By the time children enter statutory education they may have already attended a number of educational settings. Each of these experiences is likely to affect children and their capacity to adjust and to learn' (Dunlop and Fabian, 2007: 59).

The QT in this case study is part of a similar group that developed a transition programme following the publication of *Progress Matters* (DCSF, 2009), a National Strategy document that promotes good

---

practice by 'ensuring that all children make good progress throughout the Early Years Foundation Stage'. *Progress Matters* highlights the importance of sharing information with parents and professional partners, as well as the children themselves. The case study shows how to promote good practice by putting strategies into place to support children and families transitions. All Early Years settings and childminders need to share information about each child, as well as, where possible, meeting children before they transition into another setting. However, within the day-to-day work of this QT, the feedback received from both childminders and Early Years settings was that there was little or no day-to-day communication between settings and particularly between parents, childminders and settings. When discussing liaison with the school by childminders and Early Years practitioners, Hobart and Frankel (2003) suggest that schools need to understand that if childminders and Early Years practitioners are trusted by parents and have their permission to stand in for them school staff need to be trusting too. Some teachers find this difficult because they feel bound by the professional rules of confidentiality. They may require the parents' written consent to act as a proxy. The issues surrounding confidentiality and how much information schools, other settings and childminders are allowed to share can be a common dilemma.

The QT found that the transition programme in the first pre-school did not address the transitions of children who moved between settings on a daily basis and who were experiencing multiple changes of venue in any one day or over a typical week. The second setting showed how continuity of the learning and development of such children is ensured, how it is assessed and communicated and what is done to help children settle and feel secure.

Introduction to the case studies

The case study focuses on two three-year-old boys, who for the purpose of this case study are called Fred and Finn. Both are with their primary care givers (Mums) in the morning and they take them to a pre-school setting. Their childminders then collect them from the pre-school setting and care for them during the afternoon, until their primary care givers (Mums) collect them. During the afternoon the childminders take them to groups run at the local children's centres. The case studies show that the crucial elements needed to ensure smooth transitions for these children are communication and interaction between children and their adults, as well as the communication between all the adults involved with their children.

 **Fred's day**

Fred's morning was rushed as Mum had to get to work and instructions were given verbally to him – 'eat your breakfast', 'put your shoes on', 'get in the car'.

Fred was taken to pre-school by Mum and given a kiss at the door. Mum had to rush off to work. Upon arriving at the setting he was reluctant to enter but was encouraged by a staff member. Fred went to an activity but was re-directed to the carpet where he sat and waited for the other children to arrive. His comforter was removed and placed away from him. The structure of the morning was mainly adult directed and the child had little choice in his own learning. He 'got in trouble' a couple of times as he wasn't doing what he was supposed to be doing, but he loved to play with the trains and they were just over there and if he could just have five minutes there. Once he had engaged in an activity of his choice it was 'tidy up time' and he was told to sit on the carpet because all the 'mummies' were coming. Except his mummy didn't come, as his childminder arrived to collect him who had a brief conversation with the staff about him 'being fine'. The afternoon consisted of a rushed lunch and then off to the children's centre. At the end of the day Fred was collected by Mum who again had a brief conversation about him before heading home to bed.

During observation of the multiple transitions in the Fred's day, it became clear how his needs were not being met. The way adults involved in the transitions gave instructions without explanation left Fred feeling confused. They had an expectation that children will automatically remember situations and feel comfortable with them through adults giving them verbal cues. Fred had little chance to participate and to have a voice. Partnership with parents and the wider context seems absent. Communication between the adults was limited and did not focus on the needs of the child. The idea of every child being unique was not evident; for example, the adult settling Fred was not aware of his likes and dislikes. The adults failed to engage him in the setting when he arrived which is a common 'settling' technique. A transitional object is a common aid used to help settle children but Fred's comforter was taken away and placed out of reach. The pre-school routine was unfamiliar and too rigid, so Fred did not have enough time to engage in any learning opportunities. It is not clear whether the adults used strategies to communicate the transitions from context to context to Fred. The parent did not seem to be given a chance to be involved in the child's learning experiences by either the childminder or setting.

When the QT visited the setting she asked how continuity, in terms of Fred's learning and development, was being maintained. She concluded that most of the difficulties highlighted could have been easily fixed by simple communication between all parties.

 **Finn's day**

The morning started well. Mum made sure there was plenty of time to get ready and have breakfast together. She talked about Finn's day with him and shared his photo book that the setting and childminder had made together to support his understanding of his day ahead. They arrived at the setting and he was greeted by his key person. Mum was invited into the setting to support her child to settle and he was given choices about where he wanted to play. Throughout the morning he was given choices and supported by his key person. At 'tidy-up time' the model that Finn was in the middle of making was put on a shelf ready to finish tomorrow. Finn knew his childminder was coming and when she arrived the key person encouraged him to show his model to her and talk about his day. The childminder knew he liked to stop at the park on the way home and go on the swings so she asked if he would like to do this. They sat and had lunch together before heading off to the children's centre. Mum collected Finn later that day and he was encouraged to share his day with Mum. The childminder showed Mum some photos of them at the park and talked about the model he had made at pre-school, suggesting that Mum should see it in the morning when she dropped Finn at pre-school. Mum and Finn headed home together for a story before bed.

In this instance, Finn's needs were being met and there were clear strategies in place to aid transition not only for the child, but also for the adults involved. Communication was a key focus through spoken and written word as well as the use of pictures. Finn's experiences also demonstrate how giving a child choices about their day can help make them feel in control of their own transitions. The adults communicated with Finn, giving him choices, pictorial cues, audio cues and also using positive communication between his adults. These strategies ensured a good transition for Finn. The Early Years Foundation Stage (DfE, 2012) explains: 'Every child deserves the best possible start in life and the support that enables them to fulfil their full potential.' By taking care to listen to Finn, observe him and respecting his individuality it enabled him to feel valued and improved his confidence.

Much has been written about listening to the voice of the child and how practitioners can view the world through a child's eyes. In Hertfordshire an *Early Years Participation Toolkit* (2010) has been published to support practitioners to listen to children. There is also legislation in place to ensure children have a voice. This includes the Children's Act (2004), Every Child Matters (2006), the Childcare Act (2006), the Early Years Foundation Stage (2012) and the United Nations Convention on the Rights of the Child (1991). Although for both Fred and Finn the physical aspects of multiple transitions between settings still existed, Finn was supported best by better communication and closer attention to his needs. According to *Progress Matters*:

> knowledge about a child should come from a mix of observing and communicating with the child in day-to-day interactions, and information from other sources such as discussions with parents, family and other settings that the child may attend across a week. (2009: 5)

Dilemmas for the Qualified Teacher

Information sharing

In Fred's case information sharing with parents and other carers was poor. It is common for settings to give lots of written information to parents such as welcome packs and settling forms, and to ask parents for initial information they want to share about their child. The danger is that not much information sharing takes place after this initial information is collected. Parents may not be aware of the importance of children's transition experiences and may have their own concerns. 'It is also vital to recognise the role of parents and carers in supporting children at points of transition and to understand the need for reassurance, advice and support that parents and carers have at these points' (CWDC, 2010). Consideration needs to be made for parents' needs during transition times for their children and practitioners need to consider how parents may be feeling during these times. Hobart and Frankel (2003) discuss the anxieties parents may have when leaving their children with a childminder, identifying issues such as varying child-rearing practices and how cultural differences can be part of this. Practitioners who are well versed in attachment theory are better able to support parents and children during the 'settling in' process.

Communication

Effective communication is particularly challenging when children attend multiple settings. Childminders, pre-schools and primary schools need to be equally committed to good communication. Practitioners in all settings need to be seen as equally professional and any stereotypical views of childminders as 'babysitters', for instance, need to be corrected. Robins and Callan (2009) argue for working in partnership pointing out the opportunities for developing a holistic view of each child through exchange of professional expertise and development of shared values between different professionals.

Mutual professional respect

The account that follows illustrates a common occurrence.

During a transition network meeting discussing issues surrounding transition, a pre-school leader explained to the group how she had tried to contact the teachers within the local feeder infant school to discuss children's transitions. She telephoned and wrote a letter to them but received no response. In the end the pre-school delivered the transition paperwork to the infant school by hand. At the beginning of the term the infant school contacted the pre-school and asked for information on a child who had special educational needs. The pre-school leader explained how she had already sent all the information about that child. The pre-school leader expressed feelings of dismay, explaining that her colleagues had worked hard to ensure the children's transition information was sent on to the infant school but that they felt demoralised that the infant school had not acknowledged the transition information that had been prepared and sent to them and also that the infant school staff had not engaged with them. Their view was that the infant school felt they were better than the pre-school because they were 'teachers'. This was particularly concerning as the pre-school was located in a classroom *on the infant school site*.

Robins and Callan reinforce this point about services operating out of the same place. 'Just because services are "co-located" does not mean they work seamlessly together' (Robins and Callan, 2009: 73). A children's centre can be instrumental in forging positive relationships and promoting collaborative working practices between settings by being a model of good practice when working collaboratively and garnering mutual professional respect and thereby 'ensuring a co-ordinated approach which focuses on the child and their family' (Robins and Callan, 2009: 72).

Since the introduction in England of the Early Years Foundation Stage (DCSF, 2007) and the more recent revised EYFS (DfE, 2012) all professionals working with children under five have to work with the same expectations. In the past this has not been true and Early Years practitioners had separate and different frameworks to work with in the form of Curriculum Guidance for the Foundation Stage (2000), which was statutory framework, and Birth to Three Matters (2003) which was non-statutory. This schism may have encouraged teachers to think practitioners working with non-statutory guid-ance were just providing a place to play rather than a learning environment and led to lack of mutual professional respect. The aim is that every full day-care setting will be graduate led and to this end Early Years Professional Status is funded. With the intro-duction of the EYFS (2007) and its revised version (2012) and pro-fessional qualifications becoming more prominent in those working with under-fives, perhaps opinions and attitudes will shift and mutual professional respect and partnership working become the norm so that communication and information sharing comes naturally.

The Qualified Teacher's perspective

The needs of families vary. Many settings offer flexible entitlement to support the needs of working families. Settings are becoming more aware of the need to work closely with parents and give them a voice in their children's care and education. Parents need to understand their children's transitions and how they can prepare them and themselves for the experience. Perhaps children's centres or pre-school settings could run support workshops for parents to explain how they can support their child with transition and the importance of settling their children and thus ease parent's own insecurities? If parents and practitioners can ensure children experience positive transitions they will be supporting them to build up resilience and develop their ability to cope with unexpected changes they may face in later life.

Reflections

There are important leadership issues regarding children's transitions. Good practice includes positive communication between adults, ensuring the child's voice is recognised, partnership with parents, mutual professional respect and recognition and the sharing of vital information about the children going through transition. However, ensuring this happens poses some issues. A model of good practice can be shared, but ultimately it is up to individual settings how and whether they include this in their practice. There is a need for strong leadership to promote good professional relationships and mutual professional respect between settings. Such leadership begins by all settings acknowledging the importance of transitions for the well-being and futures of children.

> The experiences of children in their early years are critical determinants of future progress and attainment educationally, economically and as a member of their social community ... This means paying serious attention to ensuring the quality of experience for the child as they transfer across an increasing number of settings in their early years. (Dunlop and Fabian, 2002: xiii)

Stop Press! Update on the case study

The QT continues to evaluate transitions for children under five across the town in which she works. A town-wide project has been rolled out to all Private, Voluntary and Independent (PVI) settings, childminders and schools involving a transition process where practitioners are invited to visit children who are going to be transitioning as well as sharing of learning journals and practitioner knowledge of their children and families. The regular transition networks held across the town support practitioners in building relationships and sharing good practice. As a result the QT has begun to work alongside other children's centres in the county to support them in reflecting on children's transitions and how they can be improved. The QT is looking at how to develop a 'tool' that will support transitions for all children from birth onwards to ensure all professionals working with each family collaborate and share information.

Further Reading

Early Years is developing and changing all the time. The Early Years Foundation Stage (2007) has impacted on the practice leading up to the transition work discussed in this chapter. The Early Years Foundation Stage (2012) is the most recent framework and will become statutory from September 2012. For the most recent developments in Early Years and current government policy see www.education.gov.uk.

Fitzgerald, D. and Kay, J. (2007) *Working Together in Children's Services*. Abingdon: Routledge/David Fulton.

The need for effective multi-disciplinary teamwork and interagency co-operation across all education and care settings remains as pressing as ever. This book looks at working in multi-disciplinary teams and the challenges this may pose. It addresses a range of theoretical perspectives and contexts to stimulate students' and practitioners' critical thinking about the issues of multi-agency working.

Robins, A. and Callan, S. (eds) (2009) *Managing Early Years Settings: Supporting and Leading Teams*. London: Sage.

Because this book uses case studies and discussion points to support good practice in managing Early Years teams it is useful when someone has responsibility for children's transitions. Grounded in practice, this book puts children and families at the centre of good Early Years management. There is now considerable emphasis on such skills in this sector as the workforce becomes increasingly professionalised.

Into a crèche

Helen Longstaff

Chapter Overview

This chapter explores the dangers of being complacent in our work with families and children and, in particular, in relation to transitions for young children. The children's centre manager discusses a family's attempts to use the crèche at the children's centre for their apparently confident and outgoing child and the dissonance that arose for them when he did not settle as expected. The parents questioned long-held beliefs and decisions that they had made for their child but are ultimately able to use the situation to move forward and plan for his transition to school. The children's centre manager recognises the need to work with her own team and local network of pre-schools and nurseries to challenge any complacency. The passion and enthusiasm that was shared in the early days of establishing partnership working needs to be reignited and used to examine what is working well and how practice can be further improved to ensure the best possible outcomes for young children and their families.

Introduction to the case study

The child in this case study is Thomas, aged three, who attends the crèche while his father undertakes a course at the children's centre. The children's centre manager tells how she did some work to review and evaluate the crèche provision and concluded that it was good. Later she reflects on Thomas's experience and reconsiders the crèche provision at her children's centre and begins to rethink its place in transitions for the children. She recognises some complacency in attitudes to transition within the children's centre and the Early Years Network although the centre had already worked enthusiastically to support transition from pre-school to nursery across the area. Her fear is that, having been keen and excited about their transition work several years ago, everyone has now slipped into a comfortable feeling of 'we know how to do this', never stopping to review and consider more ways of supporting individual children and their families. The case study is related through the voices of the children's centre manager, Elaine, Thomas and his parents, Ann and David.

 **Case study**

Elaine: I already knew that I felt uncomfortable with placing a small child into crèche who may not want to be there and that we were potentially disregarding his or her needs. However, if a children's centre is expected to provide parenting courses, adult learning and other opportunities to develop for adults, suitable crèche provision is essential. I concluded that my crèche provision had to be of the highest quality and that we needed to review our provision to assess its quality.

I held a focus group with six parents where I employed an appreciative inquiry approach using a questionnaire and discussion to look at which aspects of crèche needed modifying. I then addressed specific training issues, reviewed procedures and policies, and employed a permanent member of staff to lead our crèche provision. I felt that I had taken the few suggestions for improvement seriously and that our provision was of the highest quality.

Thomas (highly distressed speaking to his parents): I didn't want Daddy to leave me. I wanted Daddy to stay with me! I didn't like Daddy leaving me.

Elaine: I had not, however, anticipated the issues that arose when Thomas, aged three, attended crèche while his father undertook a course at the children's centre. Thomas and his parents had been attending the children's centre for over two years but Thomas had never been left in any Early Years provision before. Thomas's parents, Ann and David, were interviewed at the end of the six-week period, when they gave a retrospective view of how they were feeling before Thomas attended crèche (which they chose to call 'nursery' to help Thomas's understanding).

Ann: Thomas has said he wants to go to nursery, so we sort of thought, well, you know he's ready for it, and it was a definite kind of parenting choice to be at home with him as long as we have been. I know a lot of his peers since they've turned two; they were into pre-school and for some it was even earlier. They went to day care when mum went back to work. And I just thought well, if a child becomes secure and confident in who they are with their parents, then they're going to be more confident when they're not with their parents.

David: I think we had the confidence, misplaced or otherwise; it's a familiar environment, he knows the people here, although the crèche people themselves were unfamiliar to him, but he knows the people generally on the site, he knows the place, he knows the toys, and certainly to me, it hadn't really occurred to me that he could find himself feeling stranded or whatever it was he was feeling, angry ... I hadn't prepared myself at all for the fact that he may not enjoy it to the extent he didn't enjoy it. I thought he might be a bit upset, or confused about ... 'Well, hang on, where are Mummy and Daddy?' because we've always been there.

Elaine: At the children's centre, we had not anticipated any issues in settling Thomas into crèche as we had just undertaken the review and were confident that our crèche provision was of the highest quality; however, our complacency was challenged by Thomas's very evident distress each week.

Sometime later

Elaine: Over the period of the six-week course, I had weekly contact with Thomas's parents and we agreed strategies and measures to try to address the situation. However, it became clear that the issue was related to Thomas being left without them, rather than anything within crèche. His parents talked with him after each crèche session, giving him opportunities to share with them anything that was contributing to his unhappiness. Ann and David told me that, even when prompted slightly, there was nothing that Thomas could tell them that was causing his distress other than not wanting to be left by his Daddy.

Thomas was given a camera to take photos of what he liked or did not like about the children's centre and he took many photos on the walk to the children's centre, inside and outside the building, all of which were things that he liked. Again, his only comments when asked if there was anything he did not like was that he did not want Daddy to leave him. I saw how emotional and turbulent the situation was for the whole family.

David: Having made decisions early on in Thomas's life relating to work and parenting, we fully expected our confident child to settle easily into crèche provision at a familiar setting. This, however, was not the case and we recognise that we ourselves went through a kind of transition from what

(Continued)

(Continued)

we thought was going to happen as a result of our choices and actions, to dealing with what actually happened and then planning for the future based on these events.

Elaine: I remember reading that William Bridges says transitions are split into three parts: (1) an ending, (2) a neutral zone and (3) a new beginning. He describes transitions as:

> the natural process of disorientation and reorientation marking the turning points in the path of growth. Throughout nature, growth involves periodic accelerations and transformations: Things go slowly for a time and nothing seems to happen – until suddenly the eggshell cracks, the branches blossom ... They are key times in the natural process of development and self-renewal. Without an understanding of such natural times of transition, we are left impossibly hoping that change will bypass us and let us go on with our lives as before. (Bridges, 2004: 4–5)

Applying Bridges' idea of the three phases of transition to this situation, it is clear that it is part two that caused the emotional turbulence for the family and support was needed to ensure part three was entered into as painlessly as possible. The unexpected reaction from Thomas about attending the crèche resulted in what Piaget (1997) describes as disequilibration for the family. We are often quick in our attempts to dismiss this feeling of disequilibration; however, it was a positive thing that Ann and David took time to explore their own feelings, tried to encourage Thomas to talk and shared their thoughts with me in a bid to understand what happened and to come to terms with the resulting dissonance.

Ann: We shared with Elaine how difficult this time was for us, how unexpected Thomas's reaction was and how we felt that we had not prepared him enough for his time in crèche. David and I realise with hindsight we were concerned about other parents' perceptions of our parenting choices, how Thomas would be perceived by his peers and teachers if he struggled to settle once he started at school nursery and also our own distress at seeing him so upset.

David: We had read books about separation anxiety and attachment theory when Ann was pregnant with Thomas, so we were confident that everything we had done so far in Thomas's life seemed to be ideal; he was with one of us all of the time, we were busy and active and he had opportunities to make friendships with other children of his own age. We had decided that Thomas would not attend pre-school but believed that our child would be confident and resilient when placed in crèche.

Elaine: Bowlby's attachment theory (1969) suggests that attachment provides children with a sense of security, promotes communication and the expression of feelings, acts as a secure base for children to explore their world and learn self-regulation and self-control and contributes to children's developing sense of self. I could see the strong attachment that Thomas had to both of his parents and he seemed to have a strong sense of security, his communication was excellent and he was beginning to express his feelings; he was secure and happy to engage in activities and make friends with other children and he was definitely discovering himself. However, once faced with the trauma of being left without his parents in crèche, it seemed that all of these developing skills and attributes deserted him. This disputes Bowlby's theory, even when one considers how the theory was further developed in later years to suggest that a child's attachment to other significant people in his life is as key as the attachment to the mother. Thomas seemed to be so reliant on his parents' physical presence that separation from them caused him huge anxiety, even in familiar surroundings for a relatively short period of time.

My discussions with Thomas's parents suggested that in everyday life, Thomas is given many opportunities to make choices about what he does and does not do. It was clear that when Thomas was attending crèche, he felt he had no control and he tried hard to find small aspects that he might still be able to influence or control, for example choosing where Daddy sat and holding on to certain objects that he had played with before Daddy left him in crèche.

David: When discussing control and choices with Elaine, we recognised that Thomas's emotional well-being had always been of paramount importance to us and we regularly alter what we are doing to ensure that he is happy.

Ann: So we've always kind of adjusted what we're doing and if his emotional state seems to be getting to that point where I think he's not happy ... he's just not happy here, so we just stop bringing him. But I think I was thinking well, nearly three, we need to kind of persevere with this, we need to show him that he can do it, and it just felt for me that it was a sort of trigger point, a transition point, if you like ...

Elaine: It occurred to me how confused and bewildered Thomas must have been to find that, despite the fact he clearly did not want to attend crèche, his parents continued to bring him. It seemed that this was a new experience for him as the family's usual practice was to respond to his feelings and behaviour by altering the situation to restore calm.

(Continued)

(Continued)

David: It has been good to share with Elaine how distressing this period had been for us. We are now considering whether to access pre-school provision for two or three sessions as a preparation for school nursery.

Ann: And that, I suppose, is what this whole crèche experience has opened our eyes to, well actually it doesn't matter how confident and secure he is with us, he needs to start testing that now in other situations and realise that he can do it and that he can do it without us.

Dilemmas for the children's centre manager

Two main themes arise from the case study. First, it was clear that although the transition into crèche was traumatic for Thomas, it was equally traumatic for his parents and so the centre's work with parents, and how this then in turn affects outcomes for children, is key. Second, the complacency apparent in relation to crèche may be elsewhere in the organisation and its local networks.

The distress of the child

The immediate and pressing challenge was Thomas's distress within crèche and, in addition, how this affected the other children present. As each week unfolded, different strategies were agreed and followed but the physical separation from his parents was so distressing for Thomas that all attempts to make crèche an enjoyable experience for him were unsuccessful.

The distress of the parents

Thomas's parents also went through myriad emotions during the period of the case study, from deep anxiety and concern for their son to, at times, some frustration and anger that he was unable to deal with the situation. Thomas's inability to function as the happy and confident child that they knew, merely because they were not physically by his side, was both unexpected and painful and caused them to question their key beliefs and principles in relation to family life and parenting.

Does the end justify the means?

The children's centre manager already believed that placing a small child in short term childcare provision was not necessarily in the best interests of the child but had concluded that, if she could be certain that her crèche provision was of the highest quality, then 'the end justified the means' – if adults could only access learning and other opportunities at the children's centre if care for their children was available, then short-term crèche provision was essential. However, Thomas's distress confirmed her doubts and so working with his parents to find solutions was challenging for her personally.

Could transitions be improved further at local early years settings?

The children's centre manager recognised that the adults involved were guilty of some complacency and that there was a need to explore whether this was present elsewhere in practice. Transition arrangements for young children in the local area had improved greatly due to partnership working in the Early Years Network, but was there more that could be done? Were the needs of all children being addressed, rather than just a percentage of children?

A children's centre manager's perspective

The children's centre manager found that Thomas's parents were in need of as much support and guidance as Thomas himself. As they discussed their views and feelings about what was happening, they also questioned their own competence as parents. Crèche staff also needed support and guidance as they questioned their own abilities within the crèche and considered whether the needs of other children were being fully met while they were focusing so much on Thomas.

The children's centre manager realised that a degree of complacency had crept into everyone involved: Thomas's parents had been certain that Thomas would settle easily and readily into crèche and had not stopped to question this view, while the children's centre members of staff were confident that the crèche provision was of the highest quality and that settling Thomas at crèche would be easy. The children's centre manager considered her work with the local Early Years

Network and recognised that this complacency needed challenging. The Early Years settings knew that the way they worked together was good practice and not repeated in all children's centre communities; in addition, they knew that their 'transition project work' was of high quality and was improving the transition process for local children. The children's centre manager realised, however, that they had stopped looking at what *else* could be done to support children's transitions and that to move their project forward, she needed to keep the discussion about transitions alive and current rather than allowing settings to accept the work as a finished product.

Reflections

The children's centre manager was able to use her learning from the events with Thomas in her Early Years Network and apply it to the local Transition Project which was already running well across the area. She encouraged open and honest dialogue between Early Years practitioners to explore what else could be done to improve transition from pre-school to nursery, even though arrangements were already working well. This enabled the Early Years settings to work together to identify where they could involve parents more in the process, what else they could do within the pre-schools to prepare children for their move to nursery and how they could try even harder to involve other schools and settings who had been reluctant to get involved.

Stop Press! Update on the case study

After much deliberation, Thomas's parents decided that Thomas would benefit from attending some pre-school sessions to help him get used to being without them and to develop his social skills. He is now settled and happy in reception class at school and occasionally returns to the children's centre for activities in the school holidays. The Early Years Network continues to develop the transition work and encourage other Early Years settings and schools to take part, sharing their successes and learning with other practitioners.

📖 Further Reading

Brooker, Liz (2008) *Supporting Transitions in the Early Years*. Maidenhead: Open University Press/McGraw Hill.

This book looks at the relationship between the Early Years setting or professional, the parents/carers and the child and stresses how important this inter-linked relationship is in transitions for children in the Early Years. It also looks at transitions from the viewpoint of the child and discusses different methods for capturing and listening to the voice of the child.

Edwards, C., Gandini, L. and Forman, G. (1998) *The Hundred Languages of Children The Reggio Emilia Approach – Advanced Reflections*. Westport, CT: Ablex Publishing.

The Reggio Emilia approach involves working with whole families and recognises the need to involve parents/carers as well as teachers and the environment in the child's education. This book demonstrates that support and guidance for parents and carers are key when working to improve outcomes for children.

Rushmer, R. and Pallis, G. (2002) Interprofessional working: the wisdom of integrated working and the disaster of blurred boundaries, *Public Money and Management*, October–December, 23(1), 59–66.

This journal article discusses the importance of support and guidance for professionals when building up relationships to work in new ways together. It argues that clear but overlapping boundaries are essential to support integration and partnership working.

Starting at pre-school

Amanda Ricciardi

Chapter Overview

When a parent leaves a child at a sessional Early Years setting it is a big transition for the family. The transition process in the setting is a constant feature as children start throughout the year. This has an impact on everyone: the new child, parents, members of staff and other children. This chapter explores two families' experiences of joining pre-schools with the aim of showing how transitions can be improved for future children, families and members of staff. It identifies the importance of key factors that affect transitions including the emotional well-being of the child, the quality of the preparation for the transition, the strength of key carer and family or carer relationships, and the general pre-school culture and environment.

Introduction to the case study

The pre-school in this case study provides sessional day care from a church hall. Children, aged from 30 months, attend for two and a half hour sessions for up to five sessions a week in term time only. The number of sessions children attend depends on the parents' requests and availability. Each child is assigned a key carer to welcome the family and help them settle in to the pre-school.

Case study

Oliver: Mummy walks up the ramp, holding my hand, I walk behind her and into the hall, the ladies say hello to me, I keep holding Mummy's hand and look ahead. I can see the toys on the floor in front of me and a big, tall room. We walk around the toys to a door in the corner of the big room. In my ears there is lots of chatting and laughing, it's noisy. Mummy's hand is nice and warm. We go into the long, thin room and Mummy helps me take my coat off. I look up at her as she hangs my coat and bag on the peg. There are lots of tall people and I can only see legs and a smell, like food. I look up at her, 'Blankie, Mum, blankie'. She gets it out and gives it to me. I hold her hand and in the other I clutch blankie to my chest. I walk behind Mummy into the big room. I can hear and feel people behind me, so I keep close to her legs. In the hall it is noisy again. We stand and have a look around. There are tall people talking to each other, being noisy, children on the floor playing with animals and sand. Mummy walks me over to a table, where there is some paper and paint and sponges. Mummy crouches down next to me and I lean in to be near her. The lady comes over and says, 'Hello, do you want to paint?' I start pushing the sponge on the paper and watch the big blob of paint appear underneath. Mummy watches me as I keep pushing the sponge on the paper.

Mummy says, 'See you later, Ollie. I'll pick you up, promise.' I feel very hot in my body and tears are making my face wet. I turn and reach out to her, 'No, no, stay'. I can smell her, feel her body and my body hurts. She gets very tall and I hug her legs, 'Pleeeeeeassssee'. The lady holds my hand and turns me to her. She is my size and she hugs me on her knee – it isn't Mummy's smell, warmth – she smells different. I can see Mummy walking down the hall. 'Mummy, Mummy, come back, come back.' But she goes through the door. She has gone, I want her back. I want her to come back. My blankie is in my hand and I push it onto my face. The lady is talking to me but I can't hear it. I can feel my heart beat and body going up and down on its own. The tears can't stop. My body is pushing her away from me and my legs start running to the door where Mummy went.

But a lady is there and she holds her hands out to me at the door. On the floor, I hug my body, I want her. I want her back. Now, Now. Aaarrrgggggghhhh. My body hurts. It won't stop moving on the floor. It won't stop; I can't make it stop, No. Why has she left me? Where is she? The lady comes to me and sits down next to my body and says, 'Mummy will be back soon'. I hear the lady's voice, 'It's ok, it's ok' and a rubbing on my back ... that feels nice. I can hear children playing. Some toys are near me. I look at them from the floor, but I don't want to touch them. I don't want anybody, I want my Mummy.

The floor is cold and hard and I feel sleepy. I can't hear my crying anymore and my chest is quiet. The lady is reading a book to a small child and

(Continued)

(Continued)

I listen, but don't look. I can see her body near me, her leg on the floor. The lady puts her hand on my back again and I don't move. Why has my Mummy left me here? I want my Mummy.

The lady is right next to me, she isn't talking. I sit up and look around. The room is big with lots of children, ladies and toys all jumbled up. Some children are running with a buggy. The ceiling is pointed and very far away and there is lots of talking, but I can't hear anyone. The lady is next to me. 'Would you like to have a story?' She is showing me a book. I sit next to her and she begins to read and turning the pages. I keep looking at the strangeness in front of me. Where is my Mummy? Why am I here?

 ## Case study

George: Mummy is telling me what we are doing today. She is going shopping and I am going to pre-school to see the toys, Amanda and the other children. For lunch we have ham sandwiches and yoghurt. Mummy shows me the pictures of Amanda and some of the toys they have at pre-school. We talk about the pictures and about Amanda. I like the trains and cars best. We make things at pre-school. I have a DVD about pre-school so I can watch it and show my Daddy and Nanny when she looks after me. I can show Nanny the two garages they have. Topsy and Tim went to pre-school and so did Peppa Pig. I have a book about them.

I am wearing my pre-school jumper with my new Thomas T-shirt underneath. The ladies wear the jumpers too. We are the same. Mummy says I am a big boy to go to pre-school by myself and play with the ladies and other children.

Mummy holds my hand as we walk to pre-school. Teddy is in my bag with my clothes. I can see Amanda and Sue at the door. 'Hello ... '. 'Hello,' I say, looking up. 'I got a Thomas T-shirt'. 'Oh wow, please show me.' Mummy helps me take my coat off and I lift up my jumper, smiling. I look at Amanda. She smiles too, and is kneeling down to look at the picture on my tummy. She likes it because she is smiling, I feel warm and happy. My chest feels like it will burst. Mummy says, 'Let's go and find your peg'. I look around. I see the trains on the floor as I walk past to the pegs. 'What picture is on your peg ... can you remember?' It is a giraffe. I look at the pegs as Mummy walks behind me. I can hang my own coat and bag on the peg. 'Do I want my teddy?' 'No, Amanda will get it.'

I walk with Mummy into the big hall. There are lots of grown-ups and children today.

I walk to the table, on my own, where I find my card. My card is the giraffe with a G for ... I have a look around the hall. Mummy is over by the stage. I can see her. She is watching me with a big smile on her face. I like watching the other children. Some are sitting by the sand using a spade. In the corner a child is crying and holding onto his Mummy. I walk over to the track. Mummy comes too, just behind me.

I stand and watch a child pushing the Thomas train round the track. Mummy says, 'Look there are the vehicles, which one do you want?' I pick up the long carriage and a train and sit down next to the track. I keep looking at what the other boy is doing.

Mummy is standing next to me. 'I'm going now ... see you later. I am going to do some shopping. I will pick you up and we will have some lunch together.' 'Bye Mummy.' I get up and hug and kiss her. I sit down, watching and waving at Mummy as she goes through the door. I turn to the track and start pushing the train round the track. Oh no, someone has broken it. I look around for Amanda. She comes over when she sees me looking at her. 'Amanda, look it is broken. Can you fix it?'

Dilemmas for the key carer in this pre-school

Children's emotional responses to the separation

According to Maslow (Maslow, 1943) George has regulated and internalised his emotions, having the confidence in his own identity as separate to that of his mother. A facial expression, by way of a smile was enough to reassure and confirm. Margot Sunderland (2006) argues that a child not showing any distress at the point of separation is 'holding' the emotions in and the attentive responses from the key carer are just as valid as for a child showing distress. I wonder if this is always true. Some children appear to cope naturally with a group setting.

Oliver had not acquired the strategies to part with his parents. Even though the parent had informed staff that the child's communication skills were good, his sense of overwhelming emotional loss manifested itself in a physical form as it was his more developed strategy for survival. Margot Sunderland (2006) describes this overwhelming physical response as a 'separation distress system'. The amygdala in the brain triggers an alarm response releasing stress hormones to prepare for 'fight or flight'. Over a period of time the resulting physical and emotional feelings experienced by Oliver can be calmed with a consistent, caring response. Elfer et al. (2001) suggest that distress is a normal and natural response in children who are separated from a parent and whatever the response of the child at separation it is the job of the pre-school staff to help the child acknowledge and manage the emotions.

Preparing a child for the transition

Oliver had no understanding of why he had been left (Goldschmeid and Jackson, 2004). His reaction shows how the preparation a child encounters before being left at pre-school makes a difference. According to Cole and Loftus (in McLeod, 2008) for children of this age communication of memories is triggered by external clues. In Oliver's case, apart from the key carer's name there was nothing visual for him to remember about pre-school when he was at home. In contrast a DVD and book with visually illustrated pre-school activities gave George plenty of opportunities to see and talk and rehearse in his mind how pre-school would be.

Bronfenbrenner (in Brooker, 2008) describes the importance of two-way communications. Information about the home needs to be available to the school and appropriate information about the school should be in the home. Anne O'Connor (2010) discusses the use of objects from home to help the child keep the parent 'in mind' while the child is adjusting to a setting. For both Oliver and George a 'blankie' and special toy that was especially for pre-school were used as a familiar object to keep the 'Parent in Mind' (Robinson, 2009).

The key carer relationship

The majority of the children have never been left in a group setting, making it very difficult for parents or key carers to predict how the child will respond to separation. It is also hard for a key carer to predict the parents' response to leaving their child and both parent and child need sensitive support to help manage the transition process. Initially the key carer is totally dependent on verbal information from the parent and the Initial Child Profile completed by the parent in order to make judgements on how best to support the child during their transition. Where at all possible more time should be made available with the key carer to develop the parent-setting partnership and familiarity with the child before the child starts at the setting.

This could be through visits to the setting by the child, the key carer visiting the home or even a photograph of the key carer given to the child. Eaude (2008) describes this as 'training' from the parent to help the key carer establish a rapport and link with their child. The importance of the parent as 'the lead professional' during the initial transition process must be acknowledged before the key carer/child relationship has had time to establish.

In the case studies George acknowledges the uniform both he and the key carer wear which suggests that it gives him a feeling of belonging and security. Maslow's (in Haynes and Orrell, 1993) hierarchy of needs puts 'belonging' after 'physiological and safety' and before 'esteem and cognitive' needs. This suggests that it is important that a sense of belonging is fostered in a pre-school environment as a priority. Bruner (Eaude, 2008) suggests that children of this age are Enactive (action-based) and Iconic (image-based) in their learning. Therefore how the key carer looks and what they do is important in helping the child feel secure and begin to settle.

The key carer's personal values and training are crucial. George's key carer displayed understanding and empathy for the emotions George was experiencing by staying quite close to him but she did not pressurise him to 'get over it' by distracting him or dismissing his feelings. This is 'attunement', i.e. picking up and responding to the child's needs. Parents have put their trust in the key carer and assumed she has skills that will nurture their child. Malaguzzi (in Edwards et al., 1998) talks about the importance of trust in this relationship in which the parent puts their trust in the key carer from the beginning but the child builds trust in the key carer over time.

If a transition is traumatic the sense of 'helplessness' the key carer feels may be increased. She may feel desperate wanting to make it better for the child. Her motivation may be reduced as the child may take many weeks to make very small steps of progress (Eaude, 2008). During this difficult time she may strive for vocational detachment to cope with the emotional upset and contain the child's emotions and her own (Ecclestone, 2007). Whilst the emotional well-being of each child must be considered as the most important factor for a key carer to manage during a session, difficulties in the 'settling in period' can have a detrimental effect on a key carer over a period of time. Support from other staff in the setting for the key carer can be vital. A child who becomes very attached to the key carer and seeks to be physically near at all times may find it very hard when the key carer leaves the room. A second member of staff may need to sit with the upset child on their knee until the key carer returned. This situation can be exhausting for the key carer and other members of staff have to step in to give her a break. For Oliver, the key person was essential for his welfare whereas George engaged others independently. This balance of the needs of individual children and demands of the group can place an additional stress on the key carer. If a large group of children in the room are racing around and needing constant supervision, a child may take herself off to sit away from the crowd in the corner. Staff may recognise she needs some support but there may not be a member of staff available to sit with her without jeopardising the large group's safety.

The pre-school culture and environment

For Oliver the likelihood that the environment and the presence of others would be overwhelming was unacknowledged beforehand. For George the environment was comfortable and the presence of others was prepared for and considered. Good practice requires us to design sessions to accommodate the needs of each individual child. However, the environment the pre-school occupies and the values and ethics of both staff and parents are part of meeting the child's needs too.

Teamwork between the parents and staff is essential. If parents can follow the routines and consider 'belonging' to pre-school important then their child has a better chance of developing a sense of belonging. Children who feel a sense of belonging will feel confident in their actions. George acknowledged the presence of other children in the setting and was confident self-registering and choosing an activity independently. The routine was identified by the parent as important to help the child settle and therefore George quickly became familiar with the process of beginning a session at pre-school. According to Winnicott (Pre-school Learning Alliance, 2009) social expectations are not always obvious in a new environment and this does not help to foster belonging. Expectations for both parent and child in the first 15 minutes should be clear to help a family feel comfortable.

For many children joining pre-school is the first environment they may belong to outside of the home. The environment of a 'pack away' pre-school is not ideal and may not be particularly warm or inviting. For some children the vastness of the hall can be intimidating and the entrance to the setting may be bland and uninviting, as seen with Oliver.

The key carer's perspective

A pre-school leader has important responsibilities in leading transitions. He or she should ensure all key carers feel informed, supported and skilled in order to work effectively with children and families experiencing a transition into pre-school. The importance of strategies to improve the exchange of information between the home and the setting and how crucial the parent is in the process became apparent. The key carer/parent relationship alters as the child progresses through the transition and gains a sense of belonging to the pre-school group but the parent should be viewed as a fellow professional in any Early Years team.

Members of staff have to be flexible and responsive to the child's needs and how these are manifested. Maximising the homeliness and comfort of the environment is important. For some children the most important thing they may learn while attending the setting is how to be apart from their parents. For many pre-school children this is their first independent social experience and Erikson (in Palaiologou, 2009) supports the view that children learn to cope with social realities in order to develop appropriate patterns of behaviour. Pre-school is a first of many social realities children will face in their future and if this can be positive then their capacity for further positive transitions is increased.

Stop Press! Update on the case study

The staff team has been on some staff development training that has increased their understanding that all children may make the transition of becoming a member of the group differently. The setting's greatest strength is its staff and its response to the training has deepened the caring, responsive approach that helps children and families join the setting. Other strategies have been implemented since the training such as pre-start visits, more information about the setting for parents, visual prompts for children to share at home and a change of premises to a smaller, child-friendly building.

📖 Further Reading

Clark, A. and Moss, P. (2011) *Listening to Young Children: The Mosaic Approach* (2nd edn). London: National Children's Bureau Enterprises Ltd.
This book illustrates the importance of hearing the child's point of view and how this can help practitioners provide a better service for children. When we focus on the child's point of view it really helps us to gain an understanding of how transition is experienced and how we can help the whole family during what can be a stressful time.

Lindon, J. (2009) *Parents as Partners – Positive Relationships in the Early Years*. London: Practical Pre-school.
From the start parents are crucial to help staff support and manage a child's transition to the setting. This book contains practical advice, examples of good practice and scenarios that professionals may face when establishing parent partnerships.

Robinson, M. (2010) *Understanding Behaviour and Development in Early Childhood: A Guide to Theory and Practice*. London: Routledge.
The case study showed a range of emotions from parents and children that practitioners need to try understand and respond to appropriately. This book examines the behaviour of young children in a developmental context, with an emphasis on emotional well-being. It also looks at how adults respond to children's behaviour which is an important aspect of staff development.

5

From nursery to reception

Julia Bateson

Chapter Overview

This chapter considers whether or not two primary schools, within a mile of each other, give equal support to children moving from nursery to reception, regardless of the work status of parents, and if this support influences the transition experience for children and families. It explores the first few weeks of transition through the eyes of two children in a case study. One child, Sally, is moving from private nursery to a state-sector school, and the other, Josh, is remaining at the same school but moving from nursery to reception. The case study provides an illustration of the differences in the way transitions occur depending on whether they take place within an organisation or from one setting to another. Where children attend the school nursery and pre-school, transition planning into reception is typically very good. Teachers were considerate about the children who attended their school nursery and many strategies were used to ease transitions effectively. However, we will see an example of inequality in transition support for children from other settings, for example private nurseries, other school nurseries or pre-schools. There are no opportunities for these children to experience transition sessions with their peers in the preceding term. Children who transferred to reception from other settings did not have as smooth a transition as those from within the school and were more distressed in the first few weeks. These included the children of working parents, who need full day care in order to work, and who indicated that it was a stressful process for both their children and themselves.

Introduction to the case study

Bluedell and Greendell Primary Schools are two schools about one mile apart. Each uses a different nursery to reception transition process. Both Sally and Josh live with two parents. Sally's parents both work whereas one of Josh's parents does not work. Although Bluedell School, a two-form entry school, was judged to be meeting the extended schools' full core offer, the wraparound childcare offer was only available to children from reception to Year 6. Pre-school did not tie in with nursery provision as it did at Greendell. This created a barrier for working parents, who found it difficult for their children to attend the nursery for two hours a day.

Working parents at Greendell, a one-form entry school, found it easier, as the school provides wraparound care for children from age three. This made the school a popular option for working parents but it was constantly oversubscribed, unlike Bluedell. It was common for working parents to keep their children in the Greendell pre-school or private nursery provision before transferring them to Bluedell in reception, declining a Bluedell nursery place. The exception was the children of working parents who had grandparents or childminders to take children to nursery and collect them.

One parent reported that Bluedell disallowed pre-visits for new children. On accepting a reception school place, he wrote to Bluedell to ask if his child could have some pre-visits; he was concerned since his child knew nobody at the school. The nursery teacher refused the request on the grounds of staffing and advised the parent to contact the head teacher.

At Greendell, when reception places have been allocated and accepted children from external settings are identified and contact made with their parents using a relaxed, friendly and informal approach.

A Greendell teacher said:

> We contact the parents of 'unknown' children once we have the admissions list. Parents and children are then encouraged to visit and spend some time in the nursery or pre-school group with their peers before they start.

> Wherever possible a home visit is made by the teacher who takes school photos and reception toys; meeting the child and parent in their setting reassures children so on the first school day they remember and can relate to the teacher and toys.

It is when other schools hear of such practice in a non-judgemental, relaxed environment they can reflect on their own practice and initiate positive changes in their own settings.

If Bluedell facilitated pre-visits for children transferring from other settings, in addition to parents' welcome meetings, would it enable a smoother transition? Would pre-visits encourage a child's ability to cope psychologically with their 'new situation' by getting to know and build relationships with peers and adults, understanding routines and the environment earlier?

In *The Starting School Research Project*, Dockett and Perry (2005) found that a young child's perspectives, experiences and expectations of starting school were very different to adults involved in the same transition. Sally is the focus of this case study but her experience was found to be similar to those described in Dockett and Perry. Her parents, who both work, explained that, although the build-up to the first day at school caused them concern, they thought Sally would cope because she had been at a private nursery since she was eight months old.

 Sally starts in the reception class

Sally's mum: 'So, confidence-wise, I didn't think that would be a problem and we spent quite a lot of time building up to it ... "bigging" up school.'

However, when the first day of school came:

Sally's mum: 'I really underestimated how this tiny little thing [Sally] was going into a completely different place. We'd been to one welcome meeting in the hall ... but on the day I think I was really scared, so I dread to think what she felt like.'

Sally's dad: 'She never made a fuss at all being put in a nursery for four years but it [Sally's anxiety] started straight away, dropping her off at school.'

Sally's mum: 'All your human instincts tell you, when your child is starting school, they're going to a completely different place for the first time where you're going to be leaving them in an environment with a

(Continued)

(Continued)

peer group that they've never met before; that's wrong on every level isn't it?'

Sally's parents' views imply that she had a negative initial experience, backed up by Sally's reflective comment: 'It's a bit scary when you first get there but then it's ok.'

Sally: I knew it would soon be my time to leave and move on to 'big school'. I was so excited, especially when Mummy and Daddy told me I would be going to Bluedell School in January 'cos I knew Emma went there already.

One day Mummy said I had to go to 'meet the teacher' at big school with her and Daddy. [They took a day off work.] I couldn't wait to see my new classroom and meet all of my new friends. I wondered what toys there were and if the toilets were like my nursery ones. When we got there we had to walk into a big hall full of chairs. It had a funny smell and I heard Daddy say it reminded him of when he was at school. I looked for the other children but I could only see grown-up knees and then I had to sit on Daddy's knee. 'Where are all the children? Where is my classroom and all of the toys?'

Next a lady with dark-brown hair (like my auntie's) stood up and started speaking to us but she didn't look at me and I didn't really understand what she was talking about. It was boring. Mummy gave me a biscuit to eat but I was still fed up. When was I going to see my classroom?

After what felt like ages and ages the grown-ups stood up and I had to be carried into my new classroom by Daddy so I could see above all the grown-ups. It looked *lovely*! I wanted to jump down and play with the toys. I wanted to wear a blue jumper and be like the other girls I could see in there. But then it was time to go back so I had to say goodbye. I was sad. I wanted to stay there a bit longer.

A January Tuesday three weeks later

Sally: I woke up early with a funny feeling in my tummy. My uniform was laid out on my bed and my new black shoes were all shiny by the front door. I had a new blue book bag and my name on a special sticker Mummy got for me.

I wanted to go but then I decided I wanted to stay at home with Mummy because she said she was staying at home all week this week. I was worried about who was I going to play with at school. I only knew Motty. I didn't really want to eat my breakfast. Daddy was still at home. He said he was going into work later today because he wanted to take me to school with Mummy. Daddy said I didn't have to go to school every day this week just for three mornings to help me settle in. That felt strange because at nursery I go all day long.

We all walked together, it was cold and my new coat felt really big and uncomfortable. Mummy says only half the class are here today. I looked for Motty but he wasn't there. I didn't know any of these children so I clutched my Mummy's leg and wanted the toilet.

When the door opened I saw my teacher again. She let all the mummies and daddies in with the children. It was a squeeze and it was very noisy. I started to cry and hold on tighter to my Mummy's hand. I wanted the toilet but I had to find my peg and hang up my coat first. Mummy found me the toilet right next to the peg place. I was really crying now, I didn't want Mummy to go. I saw Daddy talking to a grown-up and she came to see me. She said her name was Mrs Jooley and she wanted to look after me and show me what a lovely classroom I had. I didn't want to go with her but Mummy and Daddy said I had to. After a kiss and hug they left through the exit door and I cried and went to the window to wave goodbye. Mummy said she would come back before lunchtime. I hope that is very soon 'cos I don't have to come here tomorrow.

Wednesday

Sally: I woke up thinking, 'Is it big school today?' And then I remembered I have to go tomorrow. If I was still at nursery I would be there all day today playing with my friends and my favourite grown-ups ...

Thursday

Sally: Mummy says I have to go back to school again today. I don't want to. I want to play at home.

Sally's parents reflect on Sally's experiences:

Sally's dad: It's a big school (two-form entry). Reflecting, I suppose we should have paid a few more visits, taken Sally to the school a bit more. I think if we did it again that's what we should do.

Sally's mum: I don't know if there's the opportunity to do that though. Is there? Probably not.

Sally's dad: I don't think they encourage you to do it.

(Continued)

(Continued)

Sally's mum recollects: You get your letter from the school. We thought the welcome meeting would be child focused. It was all chairs in the hall and there were about four kids there and we thought, 'Oh, where's the children?' We thought that was a bit unusual, didn't we? But clearly for a lot of the parents there, their children were a hundred yards away in the nursery room. But there's no other option, there's nothing else you can do. You've just got to go along with the system.

Sally needing the toilet at regular intervals, and needing 'Mummy' to take her inside and then wave at the window, carried on for approximately three weeks. Mrs Jooley (teaching assistant) tried to assist when she could. After one week Mrs Jooley commented on Sally's regular visits to the toilet and it was explained that it was a 'worry habit'. The teacher had innocently put notices on the classroom window, which meant Sally couldn't wave goodbye in the mornings, triggering further distress. Sally's parents found the experience traumatic and emotional.

As a result of their experience, Sally's parents have taken a different approach with their son's transition. He will attend the school nursery one morning a week but a different private nursery three days a week. Sally's parents did not consider talking to Bluedell School about their concerns and were not aware that the school has a transition policy that states the concerns of pupils and parents are at the centre of the transition process.

A staggered first-week system

The children at Greendell start on the same day and stay all day from the first day of term.

A Greendell teacher: It's the parents we have tears from on the first day rather than the children.

By contrast, Bluedell split the class in half, alphabetically, and invite children two mornings and one day in the first week. The mornings are not consecutive; on the second morning they stay for lunch. The system is confusing for both children and parents.

The Bluedell reception teachers report that this approach gives them the chance to get to know the children better, introducing routines and carrying out assessments of their letter sounds and number work. They concede that they are aware that the children are 'dying to start school' and appreciate that parents wonder why they do it when, at nursery, they come in every day. The school's transition policy states that about 90 per cent of the school nursery children should play in the reception class throughout the previous half-term, along with providing opportunities for the reception staff to work with the nursery children, so one could argue that they have a reasonable head start, knowing the vast majority of the class before the first day of the new term.

Josh's mum: Frankly that's a complete nightmare as far as I am concerned. I think, from a parent's point of view, trying to organise your child care is very confusing ... but, separate from that I don't think it really helps the children very much. They're used to being in a class altogether in nursery, they wondered where the other half were and they also wondered, 'Now I am a big boy at school, why am I only going for half a day?' But I suspect it may be useful for the teacher to try to get to know them and that's why they do it.

Sally's mum: The most distressing part of the day is me dropping her off so, for that to happen three times as week but only get nine hours of school-ing out of it, that's a lot of stressing time for not a lot of payback time ... we didn't even get a routine. I wouldn't have said that worked particularly well with us and, also, I took the week off work so I could do the drop-offs and pick-ups and I can't take two weeks off work, so the first week of her doing normal hours I wasn't there. It mixed her up and, after that week, probably totally confused her and she probably thought, 'If this is school, it's completely different to nursery. I'm going to school for fewer hours and less days'. It completely threw her!

Sally's dad: You can see why they do it, can't you, but if the children have just come from the school nursery aren't they used to doing a couple of hours? Well, our daughter was used to doing longer days so that wouldn't have been an issue.

Another Bluedell parent: The children wonder where the rest of the class are and why they can't stay all day. I suppose this approach is helpful for the teachers but not for the children.

A non-working Bluedell parent: I think it is a good idea, as it eased my child in gently, but I think the school should give more advance notice of what happens.

Josh starts in the reception class

In this part of the case study, we look at what Bluedell did to provide Josh with such a positive experience of starting school with further insights from Josh's mother.

Josh is the second of three children. His older brother Tom is already at Bluedell. Josh's mum does not work; compared to Sally's parents, she felt relaxed about his transition:

Josh's mum: I think it made a huge difference that I had a child that had already gone through the system. The unknown quantity was not knowing how it was going to work out with this particular teacher. He's lucky, he'd been to playgroup at the school, he'd been to nursery at the school, he was quite confident in the class so that helped, I think. It helped me as well. I knew a lot of the mums; to be honest that also makes life easier. We're all in it together.

We have a very strong nursery at Bluedell – they come up very well prepared. I've heard that from other parents as well.

The first experience Sally had of Bluedell school was at the 'Meet the Teacher' session in the school hall three weeks prior to starting, whereas Josh had experienced a term of transition support. Josh was happy to move up to reception and he came to terms with the situation quickly. He had the advantage of being in the Foundation Stage unit already with familiar adults. Opportunities were provided to play in the reception classroom and playground prior to starting so Josh was comfortable with the environment and some routines. Josh did not attend the 'Meet the Teacher' meeting. He was in the nursery playing so his mum went with his sister.

Josh: Is it school today, Mummy? I really want to go … Is it today, Mummy? When can I go? Yes, yes, yes! It's today. I can wear my uniform. I will look really smart like Tom. Today I am not going to nursery because I am now in 'ception class! I can't remember my teacher's name but she's nice and there are cool toys and you get a reading book and a different playground with Year 1 and 2 and I get to eat school dinners and I might see Tom there …

Josh (later on arrival at school): Here we are, what a lot of children! Hang on a minute, I know them all from my nursery, 'cept that girl holding her mummy's leg. The teacher is letting all the grown-ups in now. *Hooray*! I know where the pegs are so I show Mummy what I have to do and I give her a kiss and tell her to go.

I go to sit on the carpet and I look at my teacher and I say, 'What's your name again?' and she says 'Mrs Bildran'. And I say, 'Oh yeah'. And I get a warm feeling in my tummy when she smiles at me. I am here at long last!

Where are my other nursery friends? They are not on the carpet. Mrs Bildran says they are coming tomorrow to settle in when I am not here. That's odd 'cos I don't need to settle in, this is my new classroom and I came in here to play a lot before Christmas ...

At playtime I make straight for the tool shed 'cos that's my favourite place and I like playing with my friends there. Tom waves at me from the big playground and I give him a thumbs up 'cos it's good here in 'ception.

After play we have a drink and a story. I like it here. I wonder what is for dinner today. I will get to see Tom too.

Ohwwwww! It's time to go home and I can't stay for school dinners – it's not fair. Why, Mummy? I don't want to go home! When can I come back? *Thursday*! That's ages. Can I stay for dinner?

In line with Bluedell policy, Josh changed from nursery afternoons to nursery mornings in the preceding term. According to Bluedell transition policy, nursery children go into their new reception class every Wednesday morning. They join the Foundation Stage assembly every Friday and Key Stage 1 assembly once a week. The reception teacher visits the nursery and reads them stories. The reception TA visits and helps with nursery play.

Josh's mum reported that Josh had established strong relationships with Foundation Stage staff before moving to reception.

Josh's mum: I knew that Josh was very safe and secure in nursery, he had an excellent relationship with the nursery teacher who also taught my older son.

Here is a letter to Santa describing Josh's experience of transition:

(Continued)

(Continued)

Dear Santa

I want to tell you that I have just started at big school and I am really excited. It's fun at school!

One of my new friends is called Sally. She says it's a bit scary when you first get there but then it is ok. Sally only knew Motty when she started because he went to her nursery. Sally likes sticking best. She likes doing art and craft with Mrs Jooley and the book corner 'cos it has books like the Gruffalo and she had that book at her nursery.

You get to wear a uniform. It is black and it is smart. You wear a blue jumper with a badge on that says 'Bluedell School' on it. I like my socks because they have fire pictures under them.

My teacher is called Mrs Bildran. When I saw her I was excited and I said. 'What's your name again?' and she said, 'Mrs Bildran', and that made me feel good. When I went in I said, 'Who are all these children?' But then I thought I know all of the children in my class 'cos they are from my nursery.

I like the office in my classroom [home corner]. It has a telephone with wires. I play in there. I am sad in the playground sometimes. One day I was walking around thinking but then I saw Pip and played with him. My favourite bit is school dinners. I like to walk there. I like to eat fish. I love walking to school with my Mummy and brother and sisters because walking is good exercise. The toilets are easy to find. The girls' is bigger than the boys' and the sinks are outside them with taps.

From Josh

Dilemmas for the Early Years Foundation Stage Leader

Even though Sally's parents accepted the Bluedell school place several months in advance, there is no evidence from Sally or her parents that the school facilitated a smooth transition or provided the same policy transition access that Josh had had. The school policy states:

The concerns of pupils and their parents are at the centre of our transition process:

- Transition should motivate and reassure children.

- Arrangements should pay particular attention to the individual needs of the children and be dependent, in part, on their age and stage of development. (Bluedell Transition Policy 2010)

It is evident that the reception teachers are very caring and work tirelessly to ensure a smooth transition for the nursery children and the new children once they start at the school. They work as a foundation unit, and work together closely, so children familiarise themselves with the environment, for up to three times a week, with an increase of classroom integration during the preceding half-term that reassured Josh and motivated his desire to start big school as soon as possible.

The big playground

Smith comments that for some young children starting school the playground was 'a daunting, frightening place, which in some cases remained so for the whole of their infant life within school' (2003: 2). If a positive adjustment is not made within the first year there could be long-term social and psychological effects. When schools develop coping strategies for young children to integrate socially within the playground, children will develop a sense of belonging, empathy for each other, and resilience against bullying and falling over. Smith recommends: school lunchtime routines to reduce children's confusion and upset; extra support to shy or lonely children, especially in the early weeks; developing the role of the lunchtime supervisor to increase their self-esteem and the quality of support for children; and a 'playground coordinator' to ensure all this happens. It was reassuring to hear from Bluedell's reception teachers that consideration had been given to this issue and strategies put in place to ease the very youngest children's transition into the main playground in the first few weeks of every term, for example the optional use of the playgroup playground (adjacent to the main playground) by reception children, who played with Year 5 designated children.

Working with other professionals

When members of the school staff observe a child struggling to settle, demonstrating quiet, withdrawn, tearful or physical behaviour they swiftly respond with support strategies and liaise with parents and psychologically ease them through transition. Where necessary they contact the school nurse or work with an Early Years local authority advisor. In extreme cases they will put the child on School Action or School Action Plus and refer to the educational psychologist. The teachers also tailor the Personal Social Health and Education (PSHE) curriculum towards the children's needs, enabling them to consider what it is like to be new at the school. For example: How might you feel and how could you help new friends when they start at Bluedell?

The staff did not link with the local children's centre. This may have been because they were unaware of the range of support services available to them, and the role the centre has, in increasing children's attainment in the under-fives. However, schools working effectively in partnership with other Extended Service professionals will improve the happiness and resilience of children and families and enhance their learning outcomes.

Parent–school relationships

Effective transition is dependent on a positive parent–school relationship. Epstein reports that the various philosophies and beliefs of teachers exemplify two main opposing theories of home–school relations. One emphasises 'inherent incompatibility, competition and conflict between families and schools and supports their separation'; the other emphasises 'coordination, collaboration and cooperation between the two' (Epstein, 1982: 85).

Adams and Christenson (2002) found that, when creating collaborative family–school relationships, parental trust is significantly higher than teacher trust. In considering wraparound care provision for pre-school children, it is not unknown to hear some teachers express the view that parents only 'use the school for childcare' whilst parents' preferred childcare options are to know their children are safe, healthy and happy and to avoid any distress and anxiety being moved between childcare settings during the day may cause. The Early Years Foundation Stage Statutory Framework (DfE, 2012) seeks to provide partnership working between practitioners and parents and/or carers. Parents who know their child's needs are being met and who feel listened to tend to trust the school. Pianta et al.'s (1995) research supported the view that children's relationships with teachers are an important component of adaptation in school.

The reception class teacher's perspective

In 2010, ACAS reported that the majority of families with dependent children have two working parents. Edelmen (2005) cites five reasons why American parents of young children go out to work apart from simply to earn money: to protect careers, for health insurance benefits, pension rights, parents' mental health and to improve children's development. Many argue that children are less likely to increase their social skills if they spend time at home with a parent/carer.

Since 2009, reports of mothers being forced back to work to try and keep family finances afloat due to the credit crunch have increased. The *Mirror* newspaper (18 April 2009) claimed that 70 per cent of mothers were feeling pressured to return to work sooner than planned.

> The recession has had a huge impact on working families around the country, with 48% of women saying they have lost their job and 8% saying they have become the main breadwinner as a result, according to a www.workingmums. co.uk poll of over 900 women. (recnews.co.uk 20)

In 2009, schools were expected to work in partnership with other agencies and professionals, known as extended services (ES). The Teacher Development Agency (TDA), now defunct and replaced by the Teaching Agency (TA), claimed that extended services would lead to parents having greater choice, flexibility, convenience and accessibility to help them balance family and work commitments. An 8 a.m.–6 p.m. offer of childcare at primary age would be a significant change for working parents, to allow for greater flexibility for parents in full- or part-time employment, supported by the ability to claim the childcare element of working tax credit, to cover up to 80 per cent of the costs.

There is an acceptance in schools that high educational standards and pupil well-being go hand in hand; that children succeed when they are happy, healthy, self-confident and well motivated. Baras (2010) states that happy parents induce happiness in their children and if children are happy, they are more likely to learn effectively. Positive emotions enable children to access higher order thinking. Unhappy, disaffected and vulnerable children find it impossible to access higher order thinking. Under stress the brain blocks the neo-cortex and the limbic system from thinking and remembered learning is slowed down or prevented (Corrigan, 2009).

A pedagogical point, supporting this argument, is made by Lee and Burkham (2002), who showed that the inequalities of children's cognitive ability are substantial, right from 'the starting gate'. Disadvantaged children start kindergarten with significantly lower cognitive skills than their more advantaged counterparts and if placed in low-resource schools, magnify the initial inequality. Therefore the smoother the transition and earlier knowledge of the child established with the reception teacher the better the chance the child has to increase their cognitive ability despite this disadvantage.

Transition

Bridges (1991) defines transition as a psychological process people go through to come to terms with a new situation and that, although change is external, transition is internal. Badly handled, transition could have lasting effects, hindering the academic, social and emotional progress of the child, a point highlighted by DfES in the publication entitled *Seamless Transitions*: '... so many adjustments are likely to have profound and long lasting effect [on the child] if the importance of maintaining coherence and continuity is not well understood' (2006a: 4).

Transition is a process, not an event. Professionals have a duty to ensure that continuity of care is as smooth as can be, a point Sanders et al. make in a study of the transition from Foundation to Key Stage 1: 'the process of transition may be viewed as one of adaptation. This study has shown that the best adaptation takes place where conditions are similar, communication is encouraged, and the process of change takes place gradually over time' (2005: 4).

If schools can support parents effectively by decreasing the stress and worry of childcare and ensuring a smooth transition to 'big school' children would be happier, healthier, more successful learners. Lack of opportunity for children from other settings for inclusion in transition sessions prior to starting could be a contributing factor to their stress and anxiety in the first few weeks. Where a school does provide opportunities for children from other settings to experience pre-visits, as was the case at Greendell, they demonstrated little or no distress and happily went straight into all-day sessions from the outset. Dockett and Perry (2005) found young children of reception age are competent, social actors, aware of their context and ability to influence as well as be influenced by their context. As a result of their findings there was increased respect amongst school communities and families for children's competence. If transition is managed well then the potential for four- to five-year-olds to deal with change happily is a reasonable expectation.

Reflections

A range of good practice recommendations may be helpful to other Early Years Foundation Stage (EYFS) professionals who are supporting transitions.

1 When schools know their reception intake they should consider contacting the parents of children coming from other settings to welcome them and arrange transition pre-visits.

2 The local children's centre is a good venue for EYFS providers to hold termly transition meetings in order to share practices, improve partnership working and increase awareness of the range of support and professionals the centre can provide in order to improve transition for children moving from other settings into school. Parent representatives can be included at some meetings.

3 Pre-visits for children new to the school organised to occur before the 'Meet the Teacher' meeting are a good idea as the children are then in a better position to 'show their parents round' their new classroom.

4 Home visits for children new to the school ease their anxiety and boost confidence. Whilst this has budget implications for schools it is a strategy worth considering as it is likely to apply to a minority of new entrants.

5 'Meet the teacher' sessions are essential because parents value the information and want to understand school expectations. It would be helpful for parents to be informed of the date and time of these meetings soon after accepting a school place.

6 Meetings at the end of the school day are easier for working parents and may increase attendance. With familiar adult supervision, children can play together in their new classroom during the meeting.

7 A staggered first week causes confusion and disruption for many families and children. Schools could consider a more flexible approach in the first weeks where parents opt for a half or full day.

8 School-dinner and playground transition strategies are effective and valued by parents and should feature in transition policies.

Stop Press! Update on the case study

Sally is a happy, high-achieving, confident learner. Emotionally she continues to need support to cope with most minor through to all major incidents of change. Her confidence has improved gradually with guidance from attentive and supportive parents and class teachers.

Josh is a happy, confident child excelling at school who copes well with change. He still adores his school uniform.

The Bluedell School now has a new head teacher, nursery and reception teacher. The head changed to one reception intake in September and, in consultation with staff, removed the staggered first week. The children remain in the same class when they move to Year 1.

A flexible approach for parents of nursery children has been adopted. They now choose which sessions their children attend. This allows working parents the opportunity to have all day care.

In March 2012, the local authority admissions team published in the local press that Bluedell School had the highest number of first-choice preferences of all the schools in the town. The school is to expand.

Greendell School continues to use the same transition process and is oversubscribed annually with a considerably smaller catchment area.

Further Reading

Adams, K. and Christenson, S. (2002) Difference in parent–teacher trust levels. implications for creating collaborative family–school relationships, *Special Services in the Schools*, 14 (1/2), 1–22.

Establishing positive relationships of trust and good communication are crucial in the transitional process. This article argues strongly for the necessity of working with parents and nursery children from other settings as soon as they have a school place accepted.

Sanders, D., White, G., Burge, B., Sharp, C., Eames, A., McEune, R. and Grayson, H. (2005) *A Study of the Transition from the Foundation Stage to Key Stage 1 Research Report, April 2005*. Nottingham: National Foundation for Educational Research (NfER).

Although it was published some years ago, this is a relevant study that reinforces many of the points made in this chapter. Transition from the perspectives of all involved, particularly the child, is helpfully analysed and recommendations made.

Smith, N. (2003) Transition from nursery to school playground: an intervention programme to promote emotional and social development, paper presented at the 13th European Early Childhood Education Research Association (EECERA) Conference, University of Strathclyde, Glasgow, 3–6 September.

The playground is a daunting place for a young reception child, a point made in the first dilemma of this chapter. This paper considers the issue and the steps schools can take to improve an experience that can put some children off coming to school.

Moving on from Key Stage 1

David Allen

Chapter Overview

This chapter explores the move children make from Year 2 into Year 3. This may be within the same school – an infant into a junior department – or it may be a transition across separate infant and junior schools. If it is the former, there are likely to be strong links along with a common ethos. This may be the same across feeder schools. It may not. The key players at this time are the class teachers, the parents/carers and of course the child. The aim, we will argue, is to facilitate effective and productive communication between all parties to ensure the child feels happy and safe, and enjoys school in order for them to learn and to develop as individuals so they can achieve their potential. This will come from careful and timely planning, allowing time for liaison and dialogue, with clear signposting and dissemination of key information. Even if the transition involves the child moving to a new class within the same school, assumptions should not be made about understandings and expectations.

Introduction to the case study

If the transition from infants to juniors is not smooth there is a possibility of long-lasting emotional damage for the child. Over time the child may well settle in and feel more comfortable but they could be deeply affected and the repercussions could last well into adulthood. An unsupported transition could also result in an achievement plateau or dip. The child may 'make up' this ground later but this cannot be guaranteed. A great deal can be done to try to avoid this and the case studies explore two possible outcomes. The first case study shows a child in the second term of Year 3 who moved from the infant to the junior department within a primary school. There was no visible support for the child or the parent prior to, during or after the move. The second child moved from a feeder infant school to their linked junior school. Measures were put in place to support the child and the family, as well as ensuring good communication between the new and existing class teachers.

 **Case study**

Beth: No one told me what would happen. No one said anything. They just let us use our imaginations. That was the worst of it – mine went wild. On the first day in September we met our new teacher, and that was scary. I was expecting a villain from a Roald Dahl book like Miss Trunchbull in *Matilda*. I was standing with my friend in the junior playground and I wasn't sure which door to go in or what the classroom would be like. We were saying, 'I wonder if they have different rules in the juniors?' We'd heard all these rumours, like you had to work through your lunch hour and that the writing books were as big as a desk. I'd never even seen a junior classroom – you only got sent to the Deputy Head's Year 6 class if you were really naughty. I didn't sleep for the last week of the summer holidays. I kept having nightmares, nothing would make them stop. I'd loved the infants and my teachers. It was small and cosy and even when we were in Year 2 we were allowed to go and help in Reception sometimes and help the little ones play with the toys. I knew there would be no toys here in the big school – I knew it would be all work, work, work! Normally, I'd talk to Mum and Dad about things but I didn't want to worry them. Besides, I overheard them having an argument about it when we were coming back from the safari park. Dad said the junior department was hopeless because they hadn't given us any information about the life and systems in the juniors. He said he had a good mind to send me into school in a dinosaur outfit on the first day because they hadn't told us what the uniform policy was. Mum said she didn't think that was terribly helpful and she was more worried that all the information about my diabetes had been passed up.

Parents' evening didn't go much better. Mrs Jones told Mum and Dad I've not made much progress since the infants, something about going backwards and then forwards so it looks like I've stayed the same. I do my best.

(Continued)

(Continued)

I just worry. I just worry all the time. Yes, I just worry. In the first term I was so busy thinking how big and scary everything was I couldn't concentrate on what my teacher was saying. I just wish I could have come and met her last year and looked at where I would be. I wish I knew some older children. I wish it was easier. I wish I didn't worry.

 Case study

Jake: It's great being in the juniors. My teacher Miss Blunn knows all about me. I met her when I was in Year 2. She came to visit us quite a bit and I even got to talk to her on my own to show her my Literacy and Maths books and I told her all about the things I like doing. She called it conferencing but it was just a chat really.

We all came to visit our new classroom as well so we would know what it is was like, ready for our first day. Mrs Blunn gave us a map too and we walked around the school to see where everywhere was. I knew already because we'd visited a couple of times to see the juniors' productions and concerts. They were brilliant – I can't wait to be in one.

The best thing was my 'buddy'. When we were in Year 2 we wrote a letter to one of the Year 3 children. Mine was to Peter and he was such a great buddy. When we came over to spend a lunchtime with a small group of my friends we ate our packed lunch in the junior dining room and then we got to play outside. I felt so grown up. It was immense. I had been a bit worried about the big Year 6 children, thinking I might get pushed around but it isn't like that. George looked after me then and he did when I came here for good in September. We still play together sometimes and he says he likes doing it because he remembers what it was like for him when he needed his buddy. I'm really looking forward to being a buddy myself. I think we could all go on a group trip to the local park – I'm going to suggest it at the next School Council meeting.

I was kind of worried about being the biggest in the infants and then being the smallest in the juniors but it isn't anything to worry about. Sometimes we do activities across the school with the older children. It's great and really feels like teamwork. There are very few problems in our playground and if there are we can go to a Peer Mediator to help sort it out. They organise games for us to play during lunchtime and come to spend time with us during wet playtimes. We've got a friendship bench too so if we're feeling a bit lonely we can go and sit there and someone will come and ask us to play.

It was so easy really, Mum and Dad and I knew all we needed to know because we came to the welcome meeting back in May last year and the Headteacher introduced us to our new teachers and explained what things were like in the juniors: what we'd need in our pencil cases, what we would get taught, homework (yawn!) and Mum got the chance to talk to Mr Roberts (he's the Special Education Needs Coordinator) about my Individual Educational Plan. Oh, I nearly forgot, we started this project in the Summer Term last year in Year 2 and we finished it off in September and when we arrived we had a massive surprise because everyone in the class had a piece of work on the wall. I felt really special. We also carried on working in the books we'd been using in the infants. Miss Blunn is always turning back to show me how much improvement I've made or with a couple of my classmates to show them what they *could* achieve. I feel like I've always been here. It's so exciting and I know I'm doing really well – Mrs Blunn says I'm exceeding my targets. Great!

Dilemmas for the Year 3 class teacher

There are five potential dilemmas highlighted in this study. The first is the need to acknowledge the different approaches and strategies of teaching infant and junior children, and finding the 'right' balance during this changeover period. The second highlights the discrepancies between assessment practices at Key Stage 1 and 2 and the potential difficulties arising from this. The third challenge relates to the perceived 'dip' in achievement of pupils in Year 3 following their end of Key Stage 1 SATs assessment. The fourth discusses the benefits of appropriate and timely communication with parents. Finally, the fifth is to evaluate the benefits of giving the children a fresh start with a clean slate.

Different teaching styles

For many infant children becoming a junior can be overwhelming. It is a 'whole new world' where new rules and systems have to be learnt, bigger spaces and equipment navigated, higher-level tasks tackled and increasingly complex relationships developed. Infant schools or departments across the globe are naturally going to be different in their approach to learning but generally, as children move away from their Nursery and Reception classes associated with sensory play, discovery learning and child-centred activities, they are more likely to experience whole-class subject teaching with a slightly more formal structure. However, resources, stimuli and

activities are still 'infant-like' and even though the lessons are challenging and differentiated the children are still in the environment
where they perceived their learning to be play. Many junior schools
have assimilated this idea and have incorporated 'play' into their
classrooms. For example using drama/role play/dressing up corners
in Year 5 and Year 6 environments to mirror infant experiences
develops amazing opportunities for extended creative writing, ICT
multimedia presentations and arts projects. The gap can be bridged
successfully.

In many infant departments there are more likely to be a greater
number of teaching assistants, nursery nurses and parent helpers
(before they step back and seemingly volunteer less as their child
becomes more independent or as they return to work). Many would
argue that this adult to child ratio should continue throughout a
child's formal education but traditionally it is here, in the infants,
that the child experiences the highest level of one-to-one with an
adult. This attention is what so often helps develop the vital foundations of the necessary skills to allow children to become independent
learners later on. Beth from the first case study commented on this
aspect saying there were fewer adults to turn to for help in the juniors
and this made her feel isolated, uncertain and alone.

Jake's teacher from the second case study acknowledged that there
were differences between the two key stages, embraced them and tried
to build links. As well as the initiatives that had been introduced to
support the transition she also made sure she had time for those traditionally infant activities throughout the year such as: carpet story
time, show and tell, play during 'Golden Time' and shared snack time
(accounting for the disappearance of funded daily fruit when the children leave the infants). There was also a slower move in Year 3 to
acclimatise the children to new teaching methods, gently removing
the high level of teacher input and helping develop independence.
Throughout the year this change was gradual so that by the Summer
Term the teaching was more 'junior' in style and approach.

The dilemma is how to allow the child to acclimatise to junior life.
The answer appears to be carefully, with support, starting in the
Summer Term of Year 2, ending in the final term of Year 3 and by
altering the teaching/learning approach and not trying to change the
child too quickly. Jake's teacher would argue that an abrupt change
as soon as they move between the year groups is not as effective.

Male teachers are few and far between in many primary schools and often non-existent in infant departments. For some children their first encounter with a male teaching role model comes in the juniors. This is an important factor and should not be underestimated. It is a huge generalisation and perhaps an oversimplification to say that all children are wary of all male teachers but it can play a part in the way an infant perceives this new environment and is important to be aware of.

During the transition it is imperative that procedures and practices find the balance between nurturing the child, instilling them with confidence and empowering them to be independent learners whilst maintaining the appropriate values, behaviour and necessary levels of mutual respect.

Discrepancies in assessments

The challenge for a junior school or department comes with the apparent disparity between the Key Stage 1 SATs and the Key Stage 2 SATs. This topic has been widely discussed in staff-rooms, Pupil Progress Meetings, conferences and online forums for many years. Some say there is a considerable disparity between the assessments. For example they would argue a Level 3 from the Year 2 SAT is easier to achieve than a Level 3 awarded by the Year 6 SAT because in Year 2 children have a higher level of support resulting in an inflated assessment. Others argue that all assessments are carefully planned and moderated to ensure continuity and complete fairness. Some junior departments carry out their own initial baseline assessments early on in Year 3 and ignore the Key Stage 1 SATs results. This perhaps does little for the high level of trust which is essential for the partnership between the two schools or departments to be effective.

However, there are ways to build the level of trust and to give both parties an opportunity to understand each school's assessment practices. Joint INSET (in-service training) between the two departments or institutions to carry out work sampling, agreement trialling* and moderation is a strong way to ensure teachers fully understand the need for common assessment procedures. Allowing teachers time and opportunity to visit their infant/junior counterpart to observe lessons or team-teach can pay dividends in the long run. Many schools now hold termly Pupil Progress Meetings to evaluate the progress individual children are making against their end of year and key stage forecast target, to discuss any needs and suggest possible interventions if necessary. The school in case study 2 ensured that the Year 2 and Year 3 teachers attended the Summer and Autumn Term meetings to open up the opportunity for healthy discussion and debate around the issue. The Year 3 teachers found they had a better understanding of where the children were academically and socially having attended the summer meeting and the Year 2 teachers gave input as to why some children may have appeared to make little or no progress (or even go backwards) in the autumn meeting.

The perceived 'dip' in achievement

What is the 'dip'? When a child is tested at the end of a key stage and achieves an externally moderated level and then moves to the next year group where they are assessed by their new class-teacher at a level lower than they had previously been awarded, this is said to be a dip in achievement. Some children also appear to plateau and remain at the same level for the whole of the next academic year. This can be frustrating for the teacher but also for the child and the parents who may not fully understand the contextual reasons.

Historically, the 'dip' has been a problem for junior schools/departments in the same way as it is for secondary schools and Year 7 teachers. It is perfectly understandable for schools to want to perform highly and aim for the best results for their children at the end of the key stage. For many this is a measure of success. Extra resources and time are likely to be put into the teaching of core subjects to prepare for the tests. This may be in the form of: extra adult support, more one–to-one teaching to boost children to achieve their potential, increased proportion of curriculum time, a certain amount of revision, preparation for the type of tasks that might be expected in the test and practise of previous papers. This all culminates in the pupil being highly prepared and at the peak of their ability. Some educationalists would argue that this is called 'teaching to the test' and doesn't fully reflect a child's true ability. Nevertheless, when they move to the next year group they do not receive this intensive support and highly focused approach to the core subjects and as a result are assessed lower than their previous best.

Often in Year 2 and Year 6 the lessons focus more intensely on English and Maths up until the May SATs to the detriment of other curriculum areas. After the tests teachers compensate by spending more time on these other subjects – completing Art and History projects, going on trips and preparing and competing in sporting activities. It is perhaps a more relaxed time where Maths and English may be neglected. There is no doubt that the yearly quota of curriculum time for these core subjects will have been fulfilled during the first nine months of the year but there is a possibility that many children won't complete much Maths and English work from May until they start the next key stage in September. This gap will undoubtedly have an effect on their level as they arrive at the next stage in their education.

The result is that in Year 3 (and again in Year 7) there is a likelihood that the children's ability will appear to have dropped. Much can be done to avoid this phenomenon and the school in case study 2 effectively employed a wide range of simple strategies to ensure this did not happen.

The teachers said that it took time, over several years, to develop the good practice by learning from each other, listening to parents, children and also colleagues in other schools to build up a robust system of support during the transition.

How to support the parents

Parents are the child's first educators; an incredible amount of learning has taken place before a pupil enters a classroom. A good infant school will recognise this and will build a strong home–school partnership where excellent communication supports the child's learning. The aim is for the junior school/department to further develop this relationship.

So why are parents likely to be worried and what can both schools do to alleviate the concern? The transition is a huge change for parents as their 'baby' is taking a visible step towards complete independence and there may be deep anxiety associated with this, albeit subconsciously. Furthermore many parents base their fears on their own experiences of schooling where support during these transitional times may have been non-existent. These feelings are often projected onto the situation with their child. All this aside, it is an innate instinct of any animal to protect its offspring. Parents want the best for their child and they want no harm to come to them, emotionally or physically. As with creatures in the wild, adults will anticipate danger, explore and evaluate a new environment to protect their young from possible threat. Humans may be more sophisticated about how they carry out these checks but the primary motivation remains the same. This is what happens as a child moves schools; parents are checking out the dangers and they want to know that the school will work effectively 'in loco parentis'. Parents need to be assured that schools are safe, inspiring places led by motivated and caring teachers who want to create a stimulating environment to develop young minds. It should be clear that even if a junior school/ department has a different approach to an infant school the aim remains constant. Imparting this message is the challenge.

Communication is key. Parents need to know that schools take their Duty of Care very seriously. Jake and his parents, in case study 2, benefited because the school made sure the channels of communication were open very early on by sending out a welcome pack with a school brochure to all Year 2 parents during the Summer Term containing all relevant information including: uniform lists, medical sheet, school-meal order forms, behaviour policy, and rewards and sanctions systems. All Year 2 parents received the junior school newsletter during their last term in the infants so they felt included in the life of the school before they even arrived. An open evening was held so the Year 2 parents could meet the Headteacher, Deputy-headteacher, class teachers, class teaching assistants, Special Educational Needs Coordinator (SENCO) and School Secretary. A presentation demonstrating the planned transition support (such as 'buddying'), including photographs/videos of school life, were shared and parents were invited to ask questions to the 'panel' and, if required, spoke to staff during a private consultation following the meeting. The infant school Headteacher also attended the evening to show the strong link and high level of communication between the schools. At the beginning of Year 3 the parents then attended a 'Welcome to Year 3' meeting with the class teachers in the classroom at the end of a school day during the first week. This paved the way for effective communication throughout the whole junior school.

A fresh start

This could be the time for a child to leave behind whatever has happened in previous years and move forward with a clean slate. A pupil exhibiting behavioural problems throughout their infant schooling may end up being labelled as a difficult child. This then stays with them when they move into the next class, their reputation travelling before them, resulting in a self-fulfilling prophesy that is nigh on impossible for the child to escape. The same can be said for children with perceived learning difficulties: 'They had lots of one–to–one guided support in the infants so it should carry on in the juniors.' This can make it difficult for the child to progress towards independence. The dilemma is how to use all the information from the infant school or department whilst keeping an open mind, making a clear decision about how to move forward and then imparting this philosophy to the child/parents. If it is appropriate they need to know that the new teacher is giving them a chance to start over.

The Year 3 teacher's perspective

It would be all too easy to let a child move from school to school or class to class with no input or additional support but Jake's teacher from case study 2 was clear that a few easily organised strategies make a huge difference. She explained that it is in her own interest as a Year 3 teacher to ensure the child is supported throughout the transition as it can make her life easier in the long run. Happy children make better learners. Jake's teacher stated that it is now a great deal easier for children to achieve their targets and this reflects well on the teachers and the schools. Instead of despairing as to how to help the child make up the lost ground because of the 'dip' she can now put her time, resources and efforts into creating a stimulating curriculum, which in turn takes the child even further. She comments: 'It's a double bonus. Everyone is a winner from a little bit of forethought and preparation.'

Since the new measures have been introduced she has to deal with fewer issues and parental concerns, particularly in the first term. She explains: 'The old adage "prevention is better than cure" is most certainly true here. As a school we try to pre-empt problems. The parents are really clear about what to expect and what we do at school. It stops them becoming anxious. This helps them to prepare their child, so support comes from all angles. I've had really good feedback, which is nice to hear.'

Jake's teacher, along with the Senior Management Team, identified a need for action and proactively introduced the current measures. Their theory was that the move had become a huge, daunting experience for the infant children and it didn't and doesn't have to be. The class teacher said one of the most rewarding parts was the joint project that spanned the infant and junior classes. A topic on 'pirates' captured the children's imagination. She team-taught with the infant teacher in July and prepared a wall display with the paintings ready for September. 'The children walked in and said "Look at my work. It's beautiful and it's up already." That made such a difference.'

It is helpful for a school to examine the current culture towards their transition procedures, evaluate their approach, communicate with teachers, children and parents and create an action plan of possible measures to trial. All educationalists are hopefully striving for the same goal: to do the best for the children. With this firmly in mind, linked schools or departments need to work towards removing any misconceptions, including the 'them and us' ideology, thus opening the staff to new ideas. Jake's teacher previously employed a strict approach for the new Year 3s which must have come as quite a shock to them. She now wholeheartedly embraces the idea of a gradual change in teaching style by easing the children into her class gently.

Reflections

In summary, the good practice in the second case study developed over time, fine tuning and adding new ideas to a model that will continue to evolve well into the future. Each cohort of children will be different, requiring different levels of attention and perhaps the employment of different strategies. However, the aim remains constant – to ensure all concerned work together to facilitate a smooth transfer, enabling the child to be happy and achieve their potential. The school established three main areas upon which to focus: support for the child, support for the parents and support for teachers.

Support for the child

The process of supporting the child through the transition is cyclic. Positive input from the teacher and parents will ultimately result in a happy, successful child and subsequently this means a degree of reassurance for the parents and professional rewards for the teacher. All parties benefit but the child remains the central concern. Jake's school from case study 2 has made sure the children know the school well by inviting them to see junior plays and productions from Year 1 onwards. They also empower the children by assigning them buddies, organising joint lunches, having tours of the school, looking at timetables, finding the toilets and comparing classroom rules. The joint project that spans the two schools helps the children realise it's really the same learning, just in a different place. They carry on working in the same Maths and English books so they, and their teacher, can look back and build on their previous learning. The Year 3 teacher spends a lesson with the class every week during the last half-term of Year 2. This is deliberately spread over a substantial amount of time to allow relationships to grow. A more intensive trial towards the end of term during previous years did not fare so well. These visits, coupled with the individual conferencing, mean the teacher is a familiar face to the child and the teacher has a well-rounded knowledge of each child. The children also spend a morning in their new class with the teacher and teaching assistant on moving on day in the last week of the Summer Term.

Children with special needs often benefit from extra visits to reassure them and eradicate worries. Photographs of their new classroom, areas of school and adults along with visual timetables and representations of school rules and systems help prepare these children for the changes they will experience. Another school adds a further sense of excitement and adventure by introducing the children to a magical character called the 'Junior Fairy' who leaves a magic wand or fairy dust on the last day of term so the children can be transformed into juniors. The whole of the Summer Term is geared towards this event and the build-up involves a great deal of awe and wonder through literacy, drama and cross-curricular work. The children are so excited about being a turned into a junior that any worries are eclipsed by this pivotal moment in their year.

Support for parents

Building up a strong relationship with the parents ideally needs to start early. In the case study the junior school weekly newsletter is sent home at the beginning of the Summer Term to give the parents a flavour of junior school life. The welcome pack containing the school brochure is sent home to the parents containing a great deal of relevant information, prior to the Year 2/3 intake evening in the Summer Term. This gives the parents time to digest the information and bring any questions they have to the meeting where they meet many members of staff and gain a wider perspective on school life. They are also shown the excellent ways the school is supporting their child through the transition. This sends a positive message to the parents that two-way communications are welcomed. To reinforce this another welcome meeting is held after school with all parents and the class teacher during the first week of the Autumn Term to revisit general information and to answer any questions. A private meeting is arranged for those parents of children with specific needs to ensure the school is well prepared and to reassure the parents.

Support for the teachers

For the transition to work effectively the school needs to fully support the Year 3 teacher by providing the necessary time and resources. This must be reciprocated in the infant school. The success of the transition in case study 2 came from open communication, active listening, diplomacy and compromise. This sense of professional trust permeates all areas of the transition: the planning of the transition topic, the moderation meetings, agreement trialling INSET sessions, pupil progress meetings, teacher/child conferencing and the meetings between Year 2 and Year 3 teachers along with both SENCOs.

In some schools/countries the teacher stays with the child all the way through their primary years (and in some countries until they are 18 years old) making any hand over unnecessary. Other schools use a system where a teacher remains with a class for two years and then a new teaching assistant joins the class in the second year and remains with them for a further two years. Using this staggered approach gives consistency for the child as an adult they know well is always able to provide support.

Stop Press! Update on the case studies

Beth from the first case study is now doing well. It took a while to settle in but she now enjoys coming to school. She is now back on track and working well towards her targets. Her parents still wish the move had been an easier one to avoid all the heartache and they have made suggestions via the Parent Forum. The school has begun to introduce measures to make the transition easier.

Jake from the second case study is going from strength to strength and is clearly flourishing at school. He is now a 'buddy' and passing on all the good things he experienced to the younger children. He is very happy, enjoying his learning and exceeding his targets.

Note

* Agreement trialling – a piece of unmarked work is levelled against agreed marking criteria by individual teachers culminating in a whole-staff discussion to agree a level to award.

Further Reading

Burgess, R. (2000) *Laughing Lessons: 149²/₃ Ways to Make Teaching and Learning Fun*. Minneapolis, MN: Free Spirit Publishing
A quotation from John Cleese 'He who laughs most, learns best' starts the first chapter of this book. It sums up the basic premise of this book – that joy and fun are an important part of childhood and by creating a happy, interesting, stimulating and laughing classroom we help promote better learning.

Galton, M., Gray, J. and Rudduck, J. (2003) *Transfer and Transitions in the Middle Years of Schooling (7–14): Continuities and Discontinuities in Learning*. Nottingham: DfES Publications.
This booklet outlines the research that should inform the way that a primary school teacher prepares children for transitions in the middle years of childhood. It looks at the 'dip' between Years 2 and 3 and how schools can prepare children for future year to year and key stage to key stage transitions.

Hayes, D. (2012) *Foundations of Primary Teaching*. Abingdon: Routledge.
This book is packed with wisdom for both teachers and trainee teachers. It recognises the importance of 'care, compassion, understanding and informed tolerance'. Denis Hayes acknowledges the importance of emotional well-being in order for children to learn and develop.

7

Adopting Steven: a chain of transitions

Alison McLauchlin

Chapter Overview

This is an exploration of the impact of transitions. The focus is on how change has affected a child, Steven, and his family. The aim is to offer the reader some conclusions from the experiences that will raise practitioners' awareness of good practice when they are working with families dealing with similar challenges and to suggest some tentative solutions for some of the challenges Steven and his family faced. In this chapter the chain of transitions that made up Steven's early years and impacted on him and his family are outlined. They include the transitions experienced when his family adopted him and when they learned that he had special needs as well as many other changes that followed in the wake of these two events.

Introduction to the case study

In this case study, the 'ups and downs' of Steven, narrated by his mother Kate, are charted and explored within their context to identify some times when Steven and his family were well supported in their transitions and the consequences of the times they were not supported well at all. The greatest transition for all of us is the moment of birth.

Unfortunately this is a transition of which Kate had very few details, although she considered herself to be Steven's mother. For Steven and Kate the transition that was the catalyst and started the domino effect of many other transitions was the adoption of Steven by Kate and her husband. They learned firsthand that the impact of unsupported transitions on their son and the rest of their family are interwoven. When they have felt supported and been able to cope this has enabled their son, Steven, to make progress but conversely where they have struggled, the 'knock-on' effect has been that his progress and well-being have been slowed down.

 Transition to become a family

Kate: Two years of attending meetings, filling in forms and putting ourselves through the Spanish Inquisition that is the adoption process were coming to a close. The adoption panel met on a Monday and, after directing a few more questions to us, they agreed that we would be suitable parents to adopt a child 0–3 years old. This in itself was quite remarkable. We had been told when we enquired about adoption that there were very few babies or young children waiting to be adopted and that only five had been placed in the county in the previous year. The statistics for 2010–2011 reflect an even worsening picture with only 60 babies placed for adoption in the whole of England (*Guardian*, 2011). Exacerbating this situation further is the increasing number of children going into care, while Children's Minister Tim Loughton (direct.gov 2012) acknowledges that the number of children being adopted is in decline, falling 15 per cent between March 2009 and 2010. There are a number of possible reasons for this. First, the length of time it takes for prospective adopters to be approved and the intrusive and rigorous nature of preparation. Only two of the five couples that undertook the preparation course with us eventually went on to adopt. Each recounted a different reason for withdrawing from the process. Second, there is a desire to establish a 'perfect match' in terms of race, age or social background, leaving many children left in the care system. Finally, there is reluctance, although understandable, by prospective adopters to volunteer to consider sibling groups, older children or those with disabilities. Overcoming these difficulties is something the current government has committed to. There is the intention to improve the adoption process to make it 'fairer and faster' as with 'every year that a child waits their chances of being adopted decreased by 20 percent' (www.education.gov 2012) so leaving many children with the prospect of remaining in care.

(Continued)

(Continued)

We had been warned to expect a possible long wait once we were approved while a child was found who would be considered a suitable match. However, the next day I received a phone call from our social worker to request a meeting as they had a 15-month-old boy who they thought would be suitable for us. They asked if I could leave work at the end of that week. What had been a very lengthy progress suddenly gathered momentum and the pace of change hardly seemed to give us a chance to pause to take a breath. Following just one meeting with our social worker and the viewing of a short video clip, it was agreed that Steven would begin the transition to be placed in our care.

Transition induction

Transition for adoption is supposed to be a staged introduction of the adopters with the child and a period to allow you to establish a relationship and develop an awareness of the child's routines and likes and dislikes. We met with our social worker and Steven's social worker and they were conscientious in their desire to have a systematic and informative induction. The value of this is advocated by Sloper et al. (2010). A timetable of the first week's meetings was drawn up and agreed to by all parties involved. The typical pattern for induction is to start with a brief meeting in the child's home, working towards longer meetings and then for the child to visit their new home, all of this taken over a period of a week to two weeks. For us the agenda agreed was slightly unconventional. On the first day we met with Steven's carers. Although we had taken two years to get to this point I do not think there is anything that really prepares you for this. The combination of elation at meeting the child who is to be your son, tangled up with the concern that you are being watched and scrutinised by the very people who are supposed to be supporting you through this process and also for us the guilt, as we felt responsible for taking a child from their birth family.

The first meeting was fairly traditional in format although we were given the opportunity to take Steven out for a walk in his pushchair. This opportunity to spend a brief time away from being watched was truly a breath of fresh air and was probably the first time we considered ourselves as a family of real people and not just descriptions on paper. Once back in his home Steven lay rolling from side to side, occasionally stretching out to reach a toy but he was unable to manoeuvre himself as he had hypotonia, low muscle tone. He appeared to seem unfazed by the arrival of all these new people and blissfully unaware of the dramatic way his life was about to change.

The second day was equally dramatic in the shift of reality that took place. Circumstances, which had been explained clearly to us, meant that unconventionally we were asked to collect Steven from his carer's home and take him to our home for the whole day before returning that evening. When this was discussed at the planning meeting with the social workers we readily agreed. I think it is fair to say that if they had asked us to put our heads in a lion's mouth we would probably have readily agreed to this too! The pressure of adoption and wanting to be seen as co-operative makes it difficult to be objective and rational. Although for us I do not think this was detrimental to the transition process, the impact on Steven must have been great; he seemed to thrive on all the attention but I cannot begin to imagine how he was making any sense of what was going on. This visit was a huge leap from our supervised visit with a ten-minute walk around the block. He was with us all day, and what seemed quite contradictory was that neither of the social workers planned to visit us on that day. We had managed to buy a car seat and pushchair, but these were about the only practical purchases that we had found the time to make in the whirlwind that requires hours of travelling backwards and forwards for induction. We decided that we needed a high chair, and so took Steven with us to the shop. Steven seemed quietly bemused by the events. His only protests seemed to be around the constant strapping and unstrapping that was required to get in and out of the car and pushchair. He probably sensed our lack of expertise. On this occasion Steven just wriggled his dissatisfaction but over the next few weeks he made his feelings increasingly clear in his behaviour.

Starting life as a family – a reality or illusion?

Steven had eczema from the very first few weeks after he was born. This may have been his body's way of demonstrating the stress and uncertainty that he was experiencing. Social workers told us that for three weeks following his birth there were many arguments culminating with his birth mother leaving the home where they were living. Steven's eczema throughout his early years has always provided us with a barometer of the feelings he was unable to articulate. Once Steven was placed with us, his carers passed on the medication that they had been using. We continued with the routine of creams and bandage wraps. Although this seemed to stop it getting worse, he still spent most of the day and all the night with socks on his hands to stop himself from scratching and making himself bleed.

We discussed our concerns about Steven's eczema with our social worker and said we would like to consult a homeopath. Whilst she acknowledged the possible benefits, as Steven was under a care order the decision had to

(Continued)

(Continued)

be made by social services. They declined our request informing us that we needed to pursue all conventional forms of medicine before they would consider homeopathy. It was frustrating to have Steven living with us 24/7 but not being allowed to make decisions about his care. Eventually Steven was seen by a consultant dermatologist who binned the medication he was on (literally). She prescribed new medication but more importantly she gave us instructions about how to differentiate between the creams and when they should be used. This information had not been passed on to us. On reflection, although a doctor for children in care had been appointed and had met with us to monitor Steven, perhaps an appointment with his previous GP might have minimised the effect of the eczema by giving us the right information at the start. I question whether it should be the role of the birth family, particularly in what is a stressful time for them, to impart medical information to the adoptive parents. This is in line with the findings of Kramer and Houston (1998) who identified that pre-adoptive parents' greatest problems were the medical and health needs of the child, raising concern that perhaps little progress has been made in over 20 years.

An unexpected transition-diagnosis

As part of the matching process we had been given a detailed document about Steven's background and development. We were aware that he was hypotonic at birth and that his physical skills were delayed. At 15 months he still needed support to sit up. We knew that this physical delay would impact on his other areas of development but there was no known cause and it was attributed to environmental factors. Prior to placement children who are to be placed for adoption undergo numerous medical tests. Steven had been tested, but because of the speed of the placement one set of results were not back; however, social workers assured us that they were not expecting anything to cause concern.

Three weeks after Steven's arrival I was asked to take him to an appointment to see his existing paediatrician. This was my one opportunity to glean as much information as possible before he was transferred to our local paediatrician. Steven appeared to respond to my anxiety, which was heightened further by being late. He hit out and pinched each time I went to manoeuvre the straps of the car seat and again in the pushchair. At the end of the appointment, the paediatrician informed me that the final tests results were now back and that Steven had a rare chromosome disorder. I was stunned. According to Sure Start (2002) the manner in which parents are informed of their child's disability or special needs comes to reflect their subsequent engagement with the support services. Steven's social worker had attended the appointment. Whilst I was grateful that she was there, my relationship with her was very limited and I wished that my own social worker was with me to offer support. I learned later that the social workers had been informed of the test results prior to the appointment. On reflection, I now wonder what my social worker could be doing that was more important than the news I was to receive. I had walked into the appointment with my son and then I walked out with my son who had special needs; this was a cataclysmic transition for which neither of us was prepared.

The experience of diagnosis of special needs is for some parents likened to going on a holiday. You pack and are prepared for a sunny holiday in Spain but when you step off the plane you discover that you have arrived in the mountainous regions of Peru with a very different climate. It is not to say you will not eventually have an enjoyable time but when you arrive you do not know where you are going, who you need to speak to get advice and feel unprepared for the terrain ahead.

Although it was a very difficult time, as the reality of the diagnosis sunk in we felt very supported by our social worker. She contacted us and gave us the option of terminating the adoption. Although we agreed that this was not an option for us, it felt a relief to be offered the choice. What we really wanted was information so that we could become more aware of the implications of our decision. Our social worker went with us to meet with the geneticists. They said it was impossible to tell us the implications of Steven's chromosome disorder as it was so rare, and that they did not want to say anything that might have a bearing on whether the adoption went ahead. As a parent this felt incredibly frustrating and condescending. Prior to the meeting I had researched about chromosome disorders and so was in a position to ask some questions. They were able to answer most of my questions clearly, despite having said they did not know anything about the disorder. They suggested that I 'should not be looking at things on the internet as that is not helpful'. However, from my perspective, my research had been very helpful, as it enabled me to ask specific questions to which they gave me some precise answers. It felt that this group of professionals were much more concerned with protecting themselves than working with us and social services in the interests of the child. However, according to Wall (2011) it may be boundaries and budgets that were hindering the inter-agency conversation.

Steven was fortunate that the rigour of the adoption process had resulted in a diagnosis for his needs. However, the label because of its rarity meant that this did not give those working to support him an indication of his prognosis. The range of needs that transpired encompassed global learning

(Continued)

(Continued)

delay, developmental co-ordination disorder (DCD) and attention deficit and hyperactivity disorder (ADHD). Throughout Steven's early years we encountered a total of 35 professionals from health, social care and education. All of these professionals were experts in their field and worked to support him. However, it was us as parents who were experts in Steven. Those who were most successful worked in partnership with us, listening and respecting our views. The greatest challenge for us, with such a range of professionals, was holding all the information from all the services in order to make the links between them. On one visit to a paediatrician in hospital I was asked to recount what the other professionals were investigating, and the results of tests that were being undertaken. I managed to recall everything, but as Steven gets older there is a lot more to remember. I now keep notes and files on everything. However, I reflected on those who we had shared the waiting area with for the last hour and wondered whether the other families all had the capability to fulfil that task.

An educational journey – the highs and lows

The transitions in Steven's education have had a great impact on Steven's emotional well-being. His first major experience of transition was attending an opportunity class which is Early Years provision for children with substantial special educational needs. I was aware of opportunity classes through my own work in education. Steven's paediatrician agreed the classes would be suitable and made the referral at my request. The way this happened typifies many of my experiences of finding appropriate provision for Steven. I would ask about and research possible provision and then, when asked, a professional was able to respond with information about a service or resource but these were not volunteered. How is a typical parent going to know what is available for a child like Steven? In fact the very best support I received as a parent was from the group of other parents of children who attended the opportunity classes. We established our own support group that met monthly throughout our children's early years. Kramer and Houston (1998) advocated that parents should be encouraged by adoption and support agencies to use these informal networks as the parents who had used them stated that they were the most helpful source of support. At these meetings we shared our experiences and invited speakers. We all said that these meetings were what helped us survive through the difficult times. This was also the place where you could share the joys and milestones that other parents would find challenging to appreciate, such as when Steven managed to jump for the first time at the age of four and a half.

A pre-school advisor liaised between the opportunity classes and the local pre-school Steven attended. This helped to maintain continuity and ensured that the existing information including his individual education plans was shared. During the transition period Steven attended both settings. The pre school was a very successful experience for Steven. He quickly progressed from spending the first session just sitting in his pushchair watching everyone to within a few weeks being eager to attend and join in all the activities. The staff adapted the activities on the mornings Steven attended to ensure he was fully included; it was a very positive experience of inclusion. This was largely down to the willingness and commitment of the staff to work with Steven. One member of staff was identified as his key worker and she built up a very positive relationship with him.

Finding a school that could accommodate Steven involved visiting local schools and talking to the head teachers to ascertain their commitment to his needs. Having chosen a school Steven was invited to the nursery for story sessions in the half-term prior to the start of his attendance. This was a good opportunity to enable Steven to become familiar with the surroundings and to meet with some of the staff. However, once at nursery the newly appointed teacher repeatedly reported Steven's negative behaviour in the setting to me in front of him. This meant he was experiencing the reprimand for his behaviour twice. The second occasion was significantly after the event, meaning he had even greater difficulties relating to it. This vicious cycle of behaviour, reprimand plus another reprimand seemed to exacerbate his behaviour. There was much shouting and hitting out at home and at school, leading to more reports of poor behaviour.

Steven's spatial awareness was one of his areas of need. As a result he did not like crowds or things close to him. Being in the small area of the cloakroom when children were collecting coats made him anxious, and he would push away anyone who got near to him. On one occasion I collected his coat and brought it into the classroom so he could put it on in a calm environment. I was told that I was not allowed to do this because Steven had to get used to using the cloakroom like the other children. This apparent inflexibility, coupled with the negative reporting of his behaviour, meant that not only was Steven very unhappy, but that I also became stressed each time I saw the teacher. Where possible, I would try to avoid coming into school or being seen by her. As someone who had been confident working in schools for the whole of my career, I felt disempowered. My experience made me wonder if parents in my situation needed an advocate to support them. I was unaware that this role could be undertaken by someone from the local authority parent partnership. It is clear that parents need professionals to provide advice in a given field but in addition they need to be able to access sensitive support when they identify a need. Carpenter suggests that:

(Continued)

(Continued)

> The reality for the family of a child with special educational needs is that they face recurrent and unpredictable challenges. Not only do they require appropriate Early Intervention, but they require access to ongoing support at points when they need to push the button. The families of children with special needs do not seek sympathy; they do not want to be patronized. They do want to be valued and treated as equals. They are not interested in being converted to particular educational ideologies or medical or therapeutic doctrines. They desire recognition of the individuality of their child and the uniqueness of their family. (Carpenter, 2007: 19)

However, on Steven's educational journey we have been fortunate to experience some amazingly inclusive teachers who have treated him as an individual, acknowledging his needs. It is the dedication and care of these that has made Steven's time so successful at the mainstream school. They made both small and significant efforts to think from his perspective, such as inviting him in briefly before school to see how the classroom had been rearranged, allowing him to assimilate the changes without the commotion that is typical in an Early Years environment. Another teacher wrote in a contact book every day to keep us informed. She always managed to find something positive to say, even on Steven's most challenging days. In addition she tried to educate both the children and other staff about how to support Steven. A teaching assistant was appointed to work with Steven and she changed classes with him, providing a constant for him and a valuable source of expertise for the class teacher. As a result of this support he developed many friendships and became very sociable. His behaviour in class improved as it was being managed very positively. For us as a family we were able to relax as the tensions experienced earlier were no longer apparent.

A reluctant transition

Unfortunately a change in head teacher marked a change of approach to Steven. I was made aware by regular phone calls that he was frequently in trouble, and the trouble escalated. Steven was required to spend much of his lunchtimes sitting outside the office. This meant that he was not able to 'let off steam' and so on his return to class in the afternoon he was already frustrated. Steven also reported that he did not like being shouted at. His behaviour both at school and at home began to deteriorate. There was shouting, hitting, kicking and throwing anything within his reach. It was a traumatic time for both Steven and the rest of the family.

The low point occurred at the time of Steven's statement review. The head teacher had made it clear in her report and at the meeting that she did not feel that the school was the most appropriate place for him, and he would be better suited to special school provision. We disagreed as Steven had made it clear that he wanted to stay at his current school and we could see that he was making progress, even if it was not in line with his peers. A report was written by the school to accompany the statement review, but as parents we did not agree with the content. There were a number of professionals at the statement review meeting including the class teacher, the head teacher, the educational psychologist and Steven's SEN officer. The meeting lasted two and a half hours, and became an unpleasant experience once we made it clear that we would not willingly withdraw our son from the school. The school stated that they had done everything they could. I was able to recommend five actions that had not previously been undertaken to provide additional support for Steven and the school. Reasons given by the school for non-implementation included 'we did not know that special schools would provide outreach' and 'we did not think it was in Steven's interest to provide this'. Perhaps if these options had been discussed with us earlier, we could have had a more positive outcome.

Parents and professionals should try to work in partnership in the interests of the child and I agree with the view that 'it is central to the notion of partnership that schools should demonstrate that they not only listen to, but also value the parents' perspectives' (Beveridge, 1997: 56). Following the meeting the recommendations were put in place. However, I do not feel that it should be the parents' responsibility to make recommendations that the school should have already actioned. Despite the school agreeing to implement these recommendations, we were pressed to state the school was not suitable. We resisted this pressure as the new initiatives had not been given an opportunity to make an impact. However, we did say that if the school felt they could not cope we would not challenge this. We offered to consider a compromise and requested that Steven be given 'dual attendance' allowing him to attend both a mainstream and a special school on a split timetable. The answer we were given was that 'county' would not consider this. On reflection, it is unfortunate that this option was so easily dismissed. The same approach had worked well to facilitate the transition between opportunity classes and pre-school. It might have eased the pressure for the mainstream school and enabled them to learn from the approaches of the special school. In addition, it could have allowed Steven to begin to form friendships at the special school. After all it was his friends that he was most concerned about missing. A chance to make new friendships during a gradual increase in his timetable at the special school might have facilitated a smooth and successful transition.

Faced with the decision and needing to make the choice about special school provision, I visited the two local schools classified as schools for children with moderate learning difficulties (MLD). I felt that whilst both would be able to

(Continued)

(Continued)

meet his needs, one catered for primary aged children only and the other for both primary and secondary aged children; the primary school was more akin to his current school and so I requested that he be allocated a place there. However, this was declined by the county as they would neither agree to pay the transport for the additional four miles that would have been required nor allow us to pay the difference. It was therefore agreed that Steven would start at the beginning of the next academic year in the allocated MLD school. A visit was arranged to take Steven to see his new school. He clearly stated his confusion about having to leave his current school, although he looked around the new school with enthusiastic curiosity. The head teacher took us on a tour and talked to both Steven and myself as we went around. When the time came for us to complete the paperwork she asked if we could go to her office. Steven was very reluctant, initially saying no, and then asking if she shouted at the children in her school. Once reassured by the head, Steven happily joined us in the office and the commitment to yet another transition was complete.

Dilemmas for Steven's mother

Who informs the parents about provision to enable fair access?

During the time that Kate ran the support group for parents and carers of children with special educational needs, all those who participated gained knowledge of some support that was available to them of which they had not previously been aware. This ranged from financial support to leisure activities. It should not be the responsibility of non-professionals to provide such crucial advice. There is the risk that well-intentioned people may provide incorrect advice. In addition, only a minority of parents choose to attend such a support group, so for all those who do not surely it should be part of each professional's role to keep the parents informed of relevant services. As the professionals involved in the case study knew about the services available and agreed that they were appropriate, parents may wonder why that information was not volunteered. One of the challenges for professionals is to gauge the most appropriate time to suggest additional services, and they may look to the parent to gain a sense of timing. Parents are all individual in their response to a child's diagnosis and so it is difficult for professionals to make that sensitive judgement. The result is that many children are not accessing support provision due to a lack of information. Well-informed parents are accessing these additional services whilst the children of parents who are not able to actively find support themselves are missing out on opportunities. These are possibly the children who may have the greatest level of need and a professional such as a key worker could be appointed to be responsible for acting as an advocate for the child and their family, liaising with the professionals involved.

The merits and risks of placing a child for adoption quickly

The time between the decision that a child should be placed for adoption and the matching of the child with adopters is on average nine months, with it taking a further month for the child to be placed for adoption (www.education.gov.uk: Table E2). The dilemmas resulting from these typical timescales could mean that potential parents withdraw from the adoption process. In addition children age, and placing older children for adoption presents greater challenges. Children may also have a prolonged stay in care, which can result in the child experiencing further disruption to their care and the professionals having to provide support for longer. If, however, the adoption process is speeded up, as is the current plan, there are possible risks that might arise. As can be seen in the case study, completing the necessary medical and background checks is time consuming but without that information adoptive parents may make a commitment that is not realistic; this may result in a rise in the number of adoption placements that break down causing further disruption and heartache to the child, parents and professionals involved. For the mother in the case study whose desire to comply with the accelerated timescale was motivated by the wish to avoid the child having yet another transition in their care provision, speeding up the process could be perceived as an enhancement to the current practice.

Who should make the decision about where a child is educated?

According to the principles of the SEN Code of Practice (2001) normally children with special educational needs will be educated in a mainstream school unless parents indicate an alternative preference. The advantage of this might be that the parents are able to take a holistic view of the child's needs, basing their judgement wholly on the needs of the child as their primary concern. It may be argued that parents are not necessarily the best informed about educational practices, or perhaps may be in denial of the extent of their child's needs, and therefore not able to make an informed and objective judgement. For the educational professionals involved, their focus is specifically on the education of the child. They need to make a decision that balances the needs of the individual with those who are educated alongside the child. This dilemma can cause a conflict for educational staff.

Increasingly, where appropriate, children are being asked to add their voice to the decision-making process. It is important that all these views are taken into account, but the dilemma arises when differing viewpoints are expressed. Ideally all parties should work in partnership to come to a unanimous decision. However, this can be a challenge as each party may come with a differing, although legitimate, agenda. Current legislation encourages the views of the parents to prevail unless the school demonstrates that it has done everything within its capability and is still unable to meet the child's needs or that the child's attendance would be to the detriment of their peers. However, if a school indicates that they are not able to meet the child's needs for one of these reasons, this as a parent presents an additional challenge. There is an option to appeal the school's decision but that would then mean parents would need to continue to work with a school that has indicated it feels unable to meet the child's needs. Does that really give parents a legitimate choice? What can ensue is a tug-of-war between the two parties with the child caught in the centre. Perhaps there is a role for an objective ombudsman to help manage this crucial decision in the transition process.

Interpreting the child's behaviour to understanding their emotional well-being

The behaviour of all children varies in relation to the context, their temperament and developmental stage. Transition is often a catalyst for a change in behaviour. It is a particular characteristic of children in their early years and children with special educational needs who might not yet have the cognitive ability, emotional intelligence or verbal skills to express their needs and so they express themselves through their behaviour. It is therefore a skill that parents and professionals need to acquire to learn to interpret the child's changes in behaviour. It may be that only by recognising and interpreting the behaviour of children are those working with the child able to provide appropriate support to maintain the child's emotional well-being.

The parents' perspective

Kate: It is difficult to distinguish where one transition started and ended as the natural flow of life has meant that we have gone from one transition straight into another. I am only too aware that we have only begun on our journey and there will be many more transitions ahead for us to face. There have been many professionals who have come along on this journey with us and Steven. My account is definitely my recollections and perspective on events and our relationships over this time; the professionals involved will have their own perspectives on the events described.

The experience has been akin to that of a dance. We have worked with many different professionals perfecting the section of the dance that is under their remit. However, we as parents are the only ones who are trying to join the sections together to make it a seamless experience for the child. The transition between each section does not flow and so the dance becomes jerky and jolted, often putting you off taking on the next challenge as you become more exhausted with the efforts required just to keep up.

Reflections

Although being part of Steven's transitions in his early years has ranged between being exhausting and exhilarating, undertaking this case study has helped to identify the themes that can be drawn out and reflect on the large number of professional who have assisted Steven to where he is now. The notions of parental choice in education, the premise of children having the right to be taught in mainstream schools, working in partnership with parents and inter-agency working as advocated by the Special Educational Needs: Code of Practice (2001) are fundamental principles and yet experience demonstrates that it is very much down the individuals involved as to whether they are adhered to successfully.

Stop Press! Update on the case study

Steven is now ten years old. He still attends the same special school, is making good progress and is looking forward to a smooth transition into the secondary department. It has proved to be a real relief to his parents to know that he is happy to stay at the school, and that he did not need to

(Continued)

(Continued)

make another major change. In his early years Steven did not like change and needed preparation if there were deviations from his normal routine. Nowadays he generally takes a change in plan in a calm and easy going manner. Steven can speak clearly and has become proficient at expressing his needs. This means his family do not need to 'read' Steven's behaviour to the extent they did before, but instead they need to find time to listen and answer his many and often repeated questions. His parents feel, as Steven embarks on yet another transition in his life, it is only through their experiences in his early years that they have learned the most effective strategies for supporting him, and know that when he is supported and happy the feeling is replicated throughout the family and their experiences will always remain closely interwoven.

Further Reading

Kirk, D. (1999) *Little Miss Spider*. London: Scholastic.
This is a beautifully illustrated book by David Kirk depicting the story of Little Miss Spider and the day that she was born. She goes searching for her mother and cannot seem to find her. She learns a wonderful lesson at the end of the book: 'For finding your mother, there's one certain test. You must look for the creature, who loves you the best!' As you can imagine it is a delight to read this book with children who are adopted.

Pugh, G. and Duffy, B. (eds) (2010) *Contemporary Issues in Early Years*, 5th edn. London: Sage.
The book provides information on current issues in Early Years. It provides clear diagrams and tables to exemplify the text. The chapters on meeting special needs, parent partnership and multidisciplinary teams were all pertinent to my experience. It was particularly interesting to note the benefits of parent partnership to the child, the parents and the practitioners.

Wall, K. (2010) *Special Needs and Early Years*, 3rd edn. London: Sage.
A great book which is written in a clear and approachable style. It covers the wide range of people that a child's special needs can have an impact upon. In addition it offers practical advice on how to work with parents effectively and as part of an inter-agency team.

Coming ready or not! A child with SEND moves up

Helena Marks

Chapter Overview

The main findings of Lamb's (2009) extensive inquiry across the special educational needs system were, first, parents need to be listened to more and, second, parents feel the whole special educational needs and disability (SEND) system needs to be more ambitious for their children. The Lamb Report recommended that the government should respond urgently to these two findings if parental confidence in the SEND system was to be increased and children's life chances improved. One of the reasons why Lamb recommends listening to parents is so they can be used as a 'window' on the views of the child by practitioners. Parents of children with SEND listen to their children's voices with their eyes and ears and through ongoing interactions on a daily basis and this needs to be acknowledged and used appropriately (Mortimer, 2004). Many practitioners, such as those working in Early Years settings, may gain high levels of trust and communication with children and their families because of their day-to-day contact with them, and this can be another effective way for all practitioners to hear the voices of children with SEND. Ofsted identifies good practice in situations where teaching assistants (TAs), working with a specific pupil with SEND, are involved in assessments and move class with the pupil to enable a successful transition to occur:

(Continued)

(Continued)

> detailed knowledge and oversight of pupil's strengths and needs, including knowledge of personal and social aspects, significantly aided the transition from one stage to the next. The pupil benefited because the TA provided a constant point of familiar reference in an otherwise changing situation. (Ofsted, 2004: 12)

In the spirit of the important recommendation by Lamb that parents of children with SEND need to be listened to more effectively, this chapter explores some of the views of parents to discover what they have noticed that makes a difference to the experience of their children during transitions.

Introduction to the case study

The case study which follows looks at the transition experiences of a six-year-old child (Gary) with Asperger's syndrome who attends a local mainstream village primary school with very little experience of SEND. During his reception year Gary had been happy and settled quite well into school. The small reception class had one teacher and one regular TA who Gary had got to know and who seemed to have some awareness of the needs of a child on the autistic spectrum. Gary's parents, Fiona and David, were being asked on a regular basis to take him home because of behavioural difficulties which some members of staff did not see as due to his SEND. School talked often about excluding Gary and had suggested Fiona and David seek an independent setting if they wanted more support. Communication was lacking between parents and school, and although Fiona and David had instigated a communication book the school said they did not have time to do this and seemed unaware of the potential benefits this could bring. The school operated a mixed-year group system and Fiona and David had expressed concerns that many of Gary's peers would move up at transition and he would then be in a class where the majority of the children would be new to him and he would be new to all of them.

 Case study

The transition from reception to Year 1 went badly, resulting in Gary being on a reduced timetable and excluded from school on a number of occasions, generally because of him hitting out at another child or a member of staff. In reception there had been one class teacher and a dedicated TA; in Year 1 there were a number of different part-time teachers and TAs, none of whom had any prior knowledge or understanding of Gary's needs. Additionally, there was no time set aside for any shared conversations between the staff and no attempt at all to involve the parents. Fiona and David spoke on a number of occasions to the head teacher but these conversations were not shared with the staff. Gary was further confused by the inconsistent use of a dedicated space that had been suggested by a visiting advisory teacher. This space was sometimes used as a punishment when Gary had behaved in a way perceived by staff as inappropriate, and at other times different staff members used it as a quiet area for working in.

Fiona: I felt that our son was struggling with all the different teachers and having to go to different classes for lessons. I went into school lots of times and talked to the head but it didn't seem that anyone was listening to me or my son or trying to understand what we were saying. Gary kept telling me that the other children were making fun of him and wouldn't let him join in their games; he said he felt cross and got a 'tingly' feeling in his tummy and sometimes he cried. When we talked to Gary it seemed these were often the times he ended up lashing out at someone because he was scared and confused.

At weekends Gary often said he didn't want to go back to school and this really upset us as parents. He talked about the little desk he had in the corner; we didn't really know why he went there sometimes as different people said different things about what it was there for and Gary just said he wanted to sit at the big tables like all the other children. We really feel that everything we said the school took as a criticism, but we just want to help them understand our son and for him to be happy at school and go all day like the other children. At home we have been taught to look for the triggers for his behaviour but we don't think the school is doing this; one teacher described having 'to battle' with our son; this really upset me.

A positive change was only achieved following the active involvement of Fiona and David through the CAF (Common Assessment Framework) process. A TAC (Team Around the Child) meeting finally took place which was instrumental in bringing all the professionals, teaching staff and parents together in order to explore what needed to change in order to improve the experiences for Gary. This facilitated and shared communication led to a greater understanding of Gary's needs by all staff, a consistent approach to supporting his needs and an increased confidence in the parents that their child was being understood and supported by all staff. The dedicated workstation was used in a consistent manner by all staff, and social stories were developed in order to help Gary understand the world around him and deal with his emotions in a more appropriate way. Additionally a staff

(Continued)

(Continued)

member who was always there was identified to be the key worker and the person who Gary knew to go to when he was experiencing difficulties; this person also became the pivotal link between home and school. Using the parents as a 'window' to the child's world had helped all the school staff to become more aware of Gary's needs and to be able to better understand any changes in his behaviour.

David: The TAC was a really big meeting with lots of people there, which was hard and emotionally draining for us. At the end of it, though, we felt that we had been listened to and that there was a much clearer understanding of our child's needs. We felt that the school had now embraced the opportunity to work with other professionals and see their knowledge and ideas as supportive and positive rather than criticism.

Having a dedicated person for us to communicate with and for Gary to go to when he felt stressed made a real difference; she helped him understand how to be with the other children and that if he was feeling angry he could tell her about it. Gary felt that she was fair which was very important given that it was his perception of injustice that in the past had caused a lot of problems.

All the staff worked together and started sharing good ideas with each other; they used a visual timetable which we find works really well at home as well. We felt that the staff had begun to see the benefits of the time spent listening to and talking with us and that we all just wanted the best for Gary.

'Social stories' have been used to help with difficult situations and increased Gary's level of understanding which has helped him to get on better with the other children and understand rules and fairness to a much greater degree. The behaviour log started to be used as a way to see where it was that things went wrong and to try and avoid these situations; previously we felt it had been used in a very negative way. We also felt that the teachers had started to look at when things went well, and use these examples to build on as a better understanding of our child's needs. The bottom line was we felt listened to and that our views and knowledge as parents were important and valued.

Dilemmas for the parent partnership adviser

Proactive communication

The overarching message from research, policy and practice suggests the experience of transition is enhanced for children and parents when there is clear evidence of communication, joined up planning and the integrated working between families and professionals. When parents are used as the 'window' through which transition experiences can be seen as if through the eyes of their child, there are better outcomes for children with SEND. Their experiences of transition benefit from active participation by parents when they are involved in this way. If there is proactive communication from practitioners and the full involvement of families including ensuring they are able to receive professional advice and guidance, transitions can be better managed so that they are less traumatic for the child and cause less anxiety to the parents. Once a 'situation' has developed, however, it is very much more difficult to re-establish trust and collaboration than if proper attention was paid to the best way of communicating from the outset. Proactive forward planning and consultation with the family, looking at how the transition can be managed to meet the needs of the child and the family before the transition occurs, is the best approach.

Mortimer (2004) looks at methods for eliciting the needs and feelings of all children and identifies the value of working with parents and carers who know their child intimately. Children with SEND may not always be able to communicate with spoken words either because they do not have that ability or they find it difficult to express their complex feelings in times of stress; instead children may demonstrate their feelings in a physical way. Often children with communication difficulties use evasive or defensive strategies such as hiding, running off, hitting or biting at times of crisis. Understanding what might be behind these behaviours is essential as a way of listening to children. Mortimer suggests that children need to feel 'licensed' to make their voices and views known, and suggests this will only happen when they feel confident. Drawing on attachment theories such as that of Bowlby (1988, cited in Mortimer, 2004), Mortimer suggests that it is possible for the adults caring for them to understand the needs of the child through actions as well as words if they are attuned to them.

Avoiding a 'one size fits all' approach

Transition is not just a physical change from one environment or context to another but includes emotional processes and experiences and psychological adjustments necessary to find a way to cope with and adapt to a new situation. Woodhead and Moss (2007) describe how children try to make sense of the discontinuities they face when going through a transition. When trying to meet emotional and psychological needs it is more difficult to plan and predict what may occur because individual experiences, perceptions and feelings fluctuate and vary enormously between and within individuals. Feelings and perceptions can also be influenced by a multitude of unknown, unpredictable and complex factors. Generalisations that lead to a 'one size fits all' approach may not necessarily achieve the best outcomes for transitions of individual children.

Taking account of differences in perspectives between the parents and the practitioner

Inge Johansson (2002) discusses parents' views of transitions to school and their influence in this process. Johansson argues that practitioners should not approach parents as a homogeneous group and further exploration of conflicts of expectations between parents and teachers is essential. Most parents feel their responsibility is to fulfil the needs of their own child. This is completely natural. However, teachers feel a broader responsibility to balance the needs of an individual child with fulfilling the needs of all children in their group. This tension needs to be specifically and explicitly explored with each family so that balancing these needs can be acknowledged as a reality. This is one of the challenges for practitioners.

Much as we may all wish otherwise, education budgets and staff time are finite. Any transition plan must take account of these factors while bearing in mind Lamb's recommendation that parents feel the whole SEND system needs to be more ambitious for their children. Practitioners need to help parents to have realistic expectations so that account can be taken of limitations of human or financial resources. If this does not happen, failure can lead to an unnecessary breakdown in relationships. When conflict between parents and professionals does occur, meeting in an open, non-confrontational way may lead to realisation that all parties have a shared interest in meeting the child's needs and re-establish trust between them.

The parents' feelings influence the child's feelings

When the parents feel secure, involved and part of the transition process, the overall experience is enhanced for their child. When parents cite positive examples of support from practitioners they are characterised by a communication process which fully involves them. Johansson explains how parental support for children during transitions is influenced by how they feel about the transition themselves.

Positive parental attitudes and well-being influence how a child adjusts to a new situation. It is not just the parents' own feelings of security that matter, it is also their level of involvement and participation in planning and enacting the transition process that influences the capacity of a child with SEND to cope. Positive feelings of parents affect the child during transitions in a very beneficial way and should be an aspiration for all practitioners.

The parent partnership adviser's perspective

For the parents of children with SEND come concerns and anxieties at times of transition that stem from lacking confidence in those in whose care you will entrust your child; this may be the first time this will be delivered by someone other than themselves. Their anxieties will not diminish if the new care givers (teachers, nursery nurses, teaching assistants) are completely unknown to the parents. Often little opportunity is given to parents to meet and establish a relationship with their child's carers prior to their children's transitions. Establishing parental confidence in the practitioners and setting in early discussions and meetings can help their children cope with the transition they are facing.

In this case study, one of the main things that made a difference and enabled the child's needs to be met was communication. Experienced practitioners know this is very often the case. Sometimes they have to work with parents trying to restore positive relationships with other professionals that have broken down due primarily to a lack of anticipatory communication. Parents may have become concerned that their children's needs are not being met and their views are not being heard. Parents' wealth of knowledge about their children should be explored and utilised by the professionals who work with their children. Other professionals who know the children well should be invited to share their knowledge. Things that work, useful strategies, ways of supporting that have been established in previous settings or at home and recognised as positively benefiting children are often 'lost in transition'. This may not be a deliberate omission but a lack of understanding of the positive benefits that working together has on outcomes for children.

Parents may feel outsiders, on the periphery of the school environment, and lack the confidence to discuss their concerns with the setting. They may assume that 'it is up to them to "get involved" rather than for schools to reach out to them' (Shields, 2009: 246). Alternatively they may assume that other people will pass on information about their child automatically to anyone who needs to know. Shields (2009: 244) notes that a number of parents in her study used negative language to describe their encounters with practitioners. For example, one parent said: 'You almost feel guilty asking a question ... you feel a little bit nervous because you don't want to be seen as a bit of a troublemaker.'

It is interesting that Shields (2009) notes that discontinuities are magnified for parents who operate outside the official discourse of education and who may be left feeling confused and excluded by the culture of the school. Once negativity has been created from an 'incident' parents can focus on what is going wrong and this perspective can become entrenched. Improved outcomes for all children with SEND will occur if a positive and constructive relationship is established from the start and a formalised process is required in which professionals access and consider parental perspectives before all transitional stages begin.

Reflections

It is important that managers take note of the time requirements of communicating effectively. Coherent exchange of information within the school is needed in order to enable communications with parents to significantly increase their confidence that their children's needs are being met. Ofsted identify poor practice as times when a number of part-time teachers and TAs working alongside a child with SEND do not exchange information and when meetings are not held regularly enough to allow staff to find time to discuss planning and assessments for the child.

Fabian and Dunlop (2006) see children, parents and practitioners as participative 'agents' in educational transitions. Fabian and Dunlop suggest there is a dynamic relationship between all three 'agents' and the social, cultural, political and policy environments in which transitions and understanding of transitions are embedded. They argue that by considering educational transitions as a relational concept, i.e. understood in terms of interactions between individuals and groups, we can gain a better understanding of what is important in transitions and a greater awareness of the effect of them on children's lives. Neuman (2002 cited in Shields 2009: 246) suggests that 'discontinuities matter because, although a good transition can stimulate learning and growth, a difficult one may have a negative impact on the child's emotional and physical health'.

This chapter has argued that interprofessional communication and high-quality partnerships with parents are important aspects of support for transitions that prevent 'discontinuities'. It has recognised that professionals may disable families, albeit inadvertently, rather than encouraging parents to share their 'window' on their child's world and promoting their skills and empowerment in terms of their children's education.

Stop Press! Update on the case study

Following a fairly settled period for Gary, unfortunately there has been a recent difficulty with a new member of staff who does not understand his needs and has said to Fiona and David that she will 'crack him'. Fiona and David feel that this teacher is struggling and feeling frustrated. They feel this was confirmed when the teacher said recently that she 'wants to win'. Once again Gary feels a sense of injustice and there appears to have been an inconsistency of approach between staff. Alongside this, the level of communication within the school appears less than ideal. The difference this time is that Fiona and David are aware of the best approach for them to take to resolve their concerns. Plans are already under way for a TAC meeting to be held as soon as possible to enable the positive benefits of open and realistic communication between all concerned, and to improve Gary's experiences of school and restore Fiona and David's confidence.

Further Reading

Jarvis, J. and Trodd, L. (2008) Other ways of seeing; other ways of being: imagination as a tool for developing multi-professional practice for children with communication needs, *Child Language Teaching and Therapy*, 24 (2), 211–27.

This article offers some specific insights in the ability to decentre and appreciate the view from an alternative perspective, highlighting the importance of this when considering, for example, those with communication difficulties who experience the world in different ways.

Turnbull, A. (2006) *Children's Transitions: A Literature Review*. Cambridge: Cambridge Children's Fund. www.cambridgeshire.gov.uk/NR/rdonlyres/0F47EDD3-B534-4319-9F8C-70870DCF42E4/0/CHILDRENSTRANSITIONS.pdf (accessed 19 April 2012).

Dr Turnbull looks at evidence suggesting that schools tend to give more attention to entrance and exit years rather than those in-between and suggest transition needs to be put more firmly on the agenda with a greater emphasis on preparing pupils for year-on-year transitions.

Vogler, P., Crivello, G. and Woodhead, M. (2008) Early childhood transitions research: a review of concepts, theory and practice, Working Paper No. 48, The Hague, The Netherlands: Bernard Van Leer Foundation.

Highlights the importance of widening perspectives on transitions in order to inform integrated and contextualised child-focused policy.

9

Receiving a diagnosis of a disability

Anne Ross

Chapter Overview

When a child is born, parents develop an image of the future for their child: who the child will be like, what they will achieve and maybe even hopes for academic success, fame and fortune. In my experience a parent when asked will almost always say that all they want for their child is to be 'happy'; a concept which is almost impossible to quantify and yet one which parents place at the top of their list of things they want for their child. With developments in antenatal scanning we can know so much more about a child before they are born, and can even contemplate surgery for correctable abnormalities before birth. Through genetic screening we can also be prepared for other abnormalities and adjustments aimed at supporting the needs of the child and family can be in place from birth. We cannot yet antenatally scan or chemically test for developmental abnormalities such as autism spectrum disorder (ASD), Asperger's syndrome (AS) and attention deficit hyperactivity disorder (ADHD). It is only after a child is born, sometimes years later, that families realise that their child is not developing as other children in their peer group are developing and they may start to question the possible causes. They look for answers and reassurances which are sometimes either slow to come forward or fail to materialise.

Introduction to the case study

The events described here happened within one family but with different siblings. The area of transition to be considered is one which affects many families seeking to understand their child's difficulties. The emphasis is on the critical transition from assessment for disability to diagnosis and the effects this has on families and children which may not otherwise be recognised by other professionals.

Family reaction to diagnosis of a disabled child is widely recognised as family members each begin working with their feelings of loss, anger, grief and isolation. However, they may also have to deal with the effects of additional non-diagnostic labels from the wider world too (such as 'bad', 'naughty' and 'useless') with its inferences on stereotyping of the parents (Fortier and Wanlass, 1984). There is no apparent evidence of the effects of no diagnosis and yet Mr and Mrs Jones were apparently experiencing strong emotional effects. Parents with and without a diagnosis for their child's behaviour are generally expected to equip themselves through parenting courses and other self-selecting interventions and often feel this again puts the blame on their abilities as parents to manage challenging behaviours in their children. The focus is invariably only on the child and his needs without consideration of the effects this is having on the whole family. Parents need time, energy and mental stability to adjust to this transition regardless of whether there is a diagnosis as a result or not (Dale, 1996). One of the most common problem-solving strategies is to seek more information (Folkman and Lazarus, 1988) and is seen as having a positive effect as a coping strategy. Sadly, there is no evidence of coping strategies for those who do not receive a diagnosis for their child following assessment and who cannot transition. There are no guidelines on the support that should be given to families who go through the process, and no final report or decision on the reasons for their child's behaviour.

 The parents look for help, support and answers

Mrs Jones made a self-referral request to our organisation to help them cope with the newly diagnosed ADHD behaviours of their daughter Jane (aged six). The professionals assigned to their case had a remit to help them cope with whatever difficulties they were experiencing and help them move forward and transition into a self-supporting family with minimal external support. The parents had recognised that they were not coping with her behaviour and sometimes their responses were inappropriate. They wanted to re-gain control in the home. They felt that Jane had taken over and was ruling them, stressing them both to the point where they feared they might snap. Her brother John (aged four) was not mentioned by his parents as being a problem or having problems but was included in the behavioural strategies introduced to make him feel more included. Yet one year later his behaviour had deteriorated to the point where the school seemed unable to cope and the parents requested a referral for a clinical assessment.

It was not a clear path through this transition. The NICE Clinical Guidelines on Autism (2011) suggest a clear pathway to assessment and aftercare; however, in this case the critical incident studied did not progress as had been expected and the NICE Clinical Guidelines had not yet been published. The parents were very keen to get an urgent appointment and they reported their hopes as follows:

1   to get some idea of what is happening and find out why he is behaving this way;
2   to find out if John has ADHD like Jane;
3   to find out if he might have something else (it had been suggested by school and the specialist support services that John might have an autistic spectrum condition, possibly Asperger's syndrome);
4   to prove that it's not their fault;
5   to be able to get him the help he needs.

Assessment

John went for assessment at the Child Development Clinic (CDC) and was initially assessed by a clinical psychologist. However, John did not appear to meet the criteria for further assessment of either ASD (autism spectrum disorder) or ADHD (attention deficit hyperactivity disorder) as expected. The clinician was therefore unable to refer him on to the consultant psychiatrist or paediatrician for further assessment. John was therefore not given any 'label' and the family was sent from the clinic with no understanding of the cause of his difficulties except the presumption by the clinician that John was copying the behaviours of his sister. When it was apparent that John would not receive a diagnosis as expected it was clear that this 'non-event' was actually having dramatic negative effects on the family and the parents in particular.

The effects of this 'non-diagnosis' were very difficult for the family to deal with. The parents reported their feelings as if they were now in 'limbo'

(Continued)

(Continued)

and had no clear pathway forward. They feared that the school would not be able to cope with the situation without a diagnosis for John and they would continue to blame him and them for his behaviour. Research suggests (Marvin and Pianta, 1996) that at this time of assessment, issues of depression among mothers is related to the stress associated to outcomes of the assessment. The relationship between children and their parents and the possibility that children will become lifelong dependants on parents can increase interrelationship issues and issues of attachment.

Effects of no diagnosis

Following this non-diagnosis event the Jones family appeared to give up and lose their strength to cope. The non-diagnosis had apparently presented them with a block to the expected transition to the next stage of support and their original hopes would apparently not now be fulfilled.

Although not clinically recognised in this situation the depression which emerged in Mr Jones was critical at this time. Mr Jones sought help from his GP and received medication to help with his depression. Mr Jones had to have time off work and reported how he felt responsible for Jane and John's behaviour. Parents may feel an underlying loss when a child has a disability or difficulty (Midence and O'Neill, 1999). When they receive a diagnosis they may experience an emotional process similar to the grieving process after death of a loved one (Bowlby, 1980). It is therefore not surprising that the Jones family described themselves as being in 'limbo'. They were stuck and could not make the transition to the next phase. Their expectations had been that John would receive a diagnosis of something and that he would then begin to cope in school and would learn and make friends as Jane had done. Mr and Mrs Jones didn't now know how to explain the situation to John. John became even less able to cope, possibly reflecting his parents' emotions and became increasingly angry and aggressive. Mr Jones's emotions were very mixed. He felt that as the clinicians hadn't been able to diagnose a disorder in John then it must be his fault as John's parent. The extent of exhibited behavioural difficulties and challenges of children with developmental difficulties are one of the most significant stressors on care givers and support staff (Hastings and Brown, 2002). Stress is a major factor on psychological well-being in parents. Bandura (1994) identified self-efficacy as the ability of a person to believe in their ability to perform and influence events that affect their own lives, and general parenting literature suggests that self-efficacy of parents has a major effect on outcomes. Mr Jones had apparently low self-efficacy in relation to his children and their needs. Bandura (1994) identified that people who doubt their abilities have lower commitment to goals and lose faith in their capabilities as a result. Mr Jones reported that he did not want to attend meetings with Mrs Jones as he felt unable to contribute. Hastings and Brown (2002) suggested a potentially high level of mental-health problems in parents of children with autism and that there were significant differences in the effects on mothers and fathers in this situation. Many studies have looked at the stressors and effects of a diagnosis of ASD in families (Montes and Halterman, 2007; Twoy et al., 2007; Pain, 1999; Fortier and Wanlass, 1984; Rivers and Stoneman, 2003; Dunn et al., 2001) and the relationship between coping before and after diagnosis in children with ADHD (McKee et al., 2004) and yet it is difficult to find any research on the effects when no diagnosis is made.

Coping strategies

Luther (2005) suggested that the ability of parents to cope was related to their ability to access effective social supports (friends, support groups, other agencies such as school nurses). Gray and Holden (1992) proposed that fathers are less likely to experience low scores for depression, anxiety and anger, and yet Mr Jones was an exception to this. He was a very active dad with his children and had been very involved in the home with their care so it is possible his attachment was higher and therefore more susceptible to these effects. The effect of all the added stress and indecision led to Mr Jones being diagnosed with severe anxiety and depression. At the same time Mrs Jones was admitted to hospital for problems with gall stones. Mr Jones then suffered a stroke which was identified as a possible result of increased stress. He was only 37 years old and was otherwise fit and healthy.

What was needed here was for Mr and Mrs Jones to receive help and support to cope with the 'limbo effect'. Unfortunately as there appeared to have been no event (i.e. no diagnosis) there was no progression through transition and no additional support (medical or educational) made available to them. A strong negative effect of no diagnosis/no transition was experienced within this family.

After many months of struggling to cope with non-diagnosis, the family situation deteriorated to such an extent that John was excluded from school on a daily basis because of his behaviour and the school's inability to meet the challenges he presented. The school felt they were not able to enforce behavioural techniques when the cause had not been diagnosed. This situation was highlighted to the education outreach support services who had been working very successfully with John's sister. The decision was made that the children needed different intervention strategies and an application was made by the support services to a local authority school specialising in social, emotional and behavioural difficulties. What John needed at this time was for someone to take action even without the diagnosis and an exception was made to the school entry criteria for him to be temporarily enrolled at this school even

(Continued)

(Continued)

though he had no diagnosis and no statement of special educational needs. The expertise within this special school enabled a more professional review and report to be issued with which the family were referred back to the CDC for another assessment. This re-assessment had been agreed because of the deterioration within the family, the apparent extension of John's needs and the professional reports from the special school. To the relief of everyone now supporting this family, the CDC consultant paediatrician confirmed a diagnosis of Asperger's syndrome. John could now access specialist support services and the family could begin to get back on track.

Dilemmas for the Specialist Coach and Family Support Worker

Working together in partnership

The TCRU report (2006) on the models of good practice in joined-up assessment within the Common Assessment Framework (CAF) recognised the importance of engaging the most effective lead professional for each individual child. The National Service Framework for Children, Young People and Maternity Services (DoH, 2004) standard 8 states:

> Children and young people who are disabled or who have complex health needs [should] receive coordinated, high quality and family-centred services which are based on assessed needs, which promote social inclusion and, where possible, enable them and their families to live ordinary lives. (Department of Health, 2004: 7)

The dilemma therefore is to enable this to happen for all families and within the CAF. One professional (TCRU, 2006), identified within the report, concluded that the effects of the CAF process had empowered some professionals in the lead professional role to access resources and maintain more control on behalf of families and young people. However, in this case study with the Jones family this did not happen. The lead professional who was the special education needs co-ordinator (SENCO) in the school had expressed at a Team Around the Family (TAF) meeting how she felt disempowered by the involvement of the social care teams, and had reported that she had no power over budgets and no options or power to increase support for the child in school as this would have had impact on the school budget. We are therefore left asking how the TAF could work for this child and his family.

The power to make change happen

The second dilemma it seems is to make change happen for families and young children within a time frame where the change can be seen as a positive experience for all those involved. The transition is the emotional response to this change and yet is often seen as the event itself. In reality a transition is a process of change which, managed correctly, has a positive outcome. Parents and professionals should consider challenging how often teams and Teams Around Children (TAC) actually look at events in the appreciative enquiry mode.

In a business setting change is a popular conception for making improvements within the workplace and yet there is always resistance. The problem is knowing what to change. The Jones family felt they were indeed in this scenario, where making change was (apparently) not within the power of anyone in the TAF. They used their apparent inability to make change happen to blame those who were not attending; the health professionals. The health professionals saw no need to attend the TAF as there was no apparent diagnosis for John and therefore their attendance did not fit their remit or their budgets. Working together requires a common vision (Fitzgerald and Kay, 2008). Perhaps the perception is that force will enable change – make parents change and the child will change as a consequence; or force the child to change through punishment and exclusion. Supporting someone through change is more achievable when we understand the barriers to change which may mean understanding the disability as well. The NICE Clinical Guidelines on Autism (2011) now suggest to parents/carers what may happen when a diagnosis is not given. The expectation for further help and support is placed on the family to pursue and there is no statutory requirement for any professional to act. The family may unfortunately, even with the most up to date legislation, still be left in 'limbo' where no help is available to make change happen. In addition it may not be within the social emotional or financial resources of the parents to move the situation forward. They do not know where to go or what to do and there appears to be no one to help as they do not fit into any statutory criteria for support. Even more concerning is that the blame for the child's behaviour is once more focused on the parents.

Providing appropriate and timely resources to the family

No matter what the cause or what the diagnosis or non-diagnosis, families need appropriate and timely resources available to them to aid their transition into the next phase of coping and moving forward with their child's difficulties. Dunn et al. (2001) suggest that stress levels in parents of children who have disability are higher than those of the neurotypical child. To wait for this support increases stress within families with family relationships deteriorating under the strain of trying to cope. In many areas of the UK children will have to wait many months from referral to assessment during which time they are unable to access statutory resources which require a diagnostic label as a qualifier. In some places the interventions appropriate to needs are only made available when there appear to be high-level indicators for safeguarding. Early intervention is the challenge, using lower-level and less costly resources to achieve a more positive and sustainable outcome for all. This is often when the specialist coach/family support worker is commissioned.

Developing a 'no-blame' culture for behavioural issues

Developing a 'no-blame' culture for behavioural issues is an essential element of teamwork. Parents report that even with a diagnosis they are often blamed for their child's behavioural issues. To ease their stresses parents need to have someone who understands what they are trying to achieve without attributing blame to anyone for past events. When developing a TAF an essential part must be the equality of all team members. Data suggests that evidenced-based parenting and family support programmes have lasting effects in improving behaviour (DSCF, 2010). Generic parenting programmes, however, increase feelings of blame in parents of disabled children as their children do not respond to generic parenting techniques, as they do for other parents in the group. Involvement in specifically tailored programmes suggests a longer-lasting and cost-effective outcome. Parents feel less isolated when working with parents who face similar challenges, helping to reduce their feelings of anxiety and inability to cope and empowering them to feel more confident in their abilities. In addition when professionals are unable to support children with difficulties they must be supported through external support services to learn alternative approaches. To blame is a waste of resources.

A Specialist Coach and Family Support Worker's perspectives

As 'professional friends' specialist coaches and family support workers work alongside families and parents and ensure they feel equal partners. The DCSF document Working Together to Safeguard Children (2010: 289) recognises that interventions work best when both parents are engaged in the process. The ability of professionals to engage effectively is vital to achieve 'buy-in' as this is seen as a 'rigorous change management programme'. The transition through assessment to diagnosis (or non-diagnosis) is perhaps more emotional than some professionals understand.

The emergence of the 'social' (social services) was historically viewed as the most appropriate way to protect children individually both physically and developmentally while maintaining the validity of the state. It was deemed inappropriate to allow the traditional patriarchal family to maintain full control of the upbringing and development of children (Dingwall and Eekelaar, 1988). Nigel Parton, in his review of this work (2000), suggests that it is now time for change and that the voluntary sector should become increasingly involved in this area with the state contributing to the funding of this work whilst ensuring inspection and regulation.

Families who engage with this specialist supportive coaching service report how social care and health professionals seem to have their own agendas for them (families and young people) to make change happen. This is not necessarily how parents or their children wish to make it happen. The challenge for professionals with a statutory remit (e.g. safeguarding, social change and health) is to get families to change when they may not want to. Having an overriding need for safeguarding but also having an autonomous working remit allows the use of coaching methods which are non-directive whilst engaging local authority commissioned funding. These methods, however, are not overly regulated which enables us to inspire, encourage and develop 'professional parents' (parents who have skills, personal experience and perspective of ADHD/ASD) to support other parents in our unique way. We work with the presumption that the client does know what to do, they just don't know they know! The emphasis is to enable the client through partnership working to identify what the challenges are and how best to approach them and then find the solutions within their own emotional and physical resources, with guidance from the coach. On reflection the difference here is that social care workers aim to make change happen whereas at ADD-vance (*a charitable voluntary organisation*) we aim to enable and empower families and young people to make their own changes happen. We need both approaches to enable all families to achieve.

Reflections

Leadership is not about telling people, but demonstrating how it can be done, and by sharing with and encouraging others to develop through example. The ethos of 'Think Family' in practice can be challenging. In the field described here little can be achieved by one person and working in partnership with others can have a dramatic effect. It is, though, important to have a clear leadership to direct and co-ordinate TAF activity.

The specialist ASD/ADHD coach and family support worker has a teaching role as well as a coaching and supporting role, teaching or advising other professionals to understand the views of the family and enabling professionals to understand the disabilities (or suspected disabilities). This often requires diplomacy, tact and time to build rapport.

Expert knowledge of ASD/ADHD enables the coach to promote best practice and intervention. In addition all coaches have personal experience of the disabilities and they have the unique position to be able to add personal experience into a professional agenda. This approach reduces barriers with parents and enables more effective partnership working with professionals.

Developing a no-blame culture between parents and professionals is a key role. For every behaviour there is always a cause and we must not assume poor behaviour in children is due to bad parenting. Professionals are often unfairly viewed as 'the enemy' by families and professionals will view parents as 'failing' or 'to blame'. The truth is that by working more closely together in a trusting relationship the TAF can achieve so much more. Professionals are trained in their specialist field and yet may need additional learning about the disabilities while parents should be accepted as experts in their own children. Parents should be seen as 'professional parents' for their own families and of equal value in a TAF.

Stop Press! Update on the case study

The situation for this family has improved considerably. John is now well settled in his special school having returned briefly (and unsuccessfully) to his original mainstream school following the diagnosis. The family are now stronger and working together. They have had an additional child who does not yet have any signs or symptoms of autism or ADHD. John has a statement of special educational needs and the TAF system has been maintained within their local authority so that the family are now being supported by a range of services in a more co-ordinated approach. The family continue to be involved in the local ASD/ADHD support group.

 Further Reading

Attwood, A. (2008) *The Complete Guide to Asperger's Syndrome*. London: Jessica Kingsley Publishers.
One of the most popular texts available, this book gives a straightforward introduction to Asperger's syndrome and is suitable for both parents and professionals

Baron-Cohen, S. (2008) *Autism and Asperger's Syndrome*. Oxford: Oxford University Press.
Excellent text by one of the world's most experienced experts in this field. A comprehensive guide for professionals and parents with case study examples.

Roth, I., Barson, C., Hoekstra, R. and Pasco, G. (2010) *The Autism Spectrum in the 21st century*. London: Jessica Kingsley Publishers.
A comprehensive guide to autism and Asperger's syndrome, diagnosis and assessment, explanations, interventions and family issues.

10

Lost in transitions!

Sally Patterson

Chapter Overview

This chapter explores the role Home-Start plays in supporting families through transitions and is written from the perspective of a manager of a local Home-Start scheme. Home-Start is a voluntary organisation whose remit is to provide support and friendship to parents who have at least one child under five living with them, in their own home. The scheme recruits and trains volunteers who are then matched with families who have asked for help. The volunteers, who all have experience of full-time parenting themselves, visit the families once a week for two to three hours. They try to help with the stresses and strains of parenting and to prevent a crisis or family breakdown. Home-Start has been in existence for nearly 40 years, and its approach to supporting families is unique. It works through parents supporting parents, it is independent of statutory organisations and the parents choose whether to accept help. Home-Start is a preventative service, and focuses on early intervention, in order to prevent a family's needs escalating. The earlier a service is put in place the better, for this minimises a child's experience of difficulties (Munro, 2011: 70).

Introduction to the case study

This case study focuses on Maria and her son Alex. Alex is a three-year-old boy who, with his mother, has gone through a series of traumatic transitions. During his three short years he had experienced his parents separating and divorcing; the loss of the family home; moving to Greece to live with extended family and learning to speak Greek rather than English; returning to England, to a new house with only his mother for company, and to a nursery school where everyone was speaking a language he did not understand. Maria was feeling isolated and struggling to cope. She wanted someone to talk to, play with her son and give her a break.

This is exactly the kind of scenario in which Home-Start is able to offer help. Home-Start believes that by helping to meet the parents' needs, it is helping the child. Thus its main objective is to support the parents (the parents are its clients) where other professionals, such as health visitors and social workers, have the child as their client and central focus.

Once a referral has been received, the family is visited and a dialogue takes place: parents tell the Home-Start co-ordinator their story and she tells them about Home-Start and what it can offer. Together they identify the areas where a volunteer may be able to help and the parents make a decision about whether or not to accept Home-Start's support.

 **Case study**

Alex: Geia sas! To onoma mow einai Alex. Eimai trion eton.

Can you understand me? No, I thought not. It is my language, it is Greek. I said, Good morning, my name is Alex. I am three years old. This morning I start nursery school. I am standing in the doorway, looking at the room, the teachers and the other children. One teacher comes towards me and smiles. 'Hello Alex,' she says. 'Welcome to our nursery. Shall I show you where to put your coat?'

I take a step backwards, closer to my Mum. The teacher reaches out her hand to me and says, 'Alex, don't be worried. You'll make lots of friends here and have fun playing with the toys.'

Do you understand what she said? I don't. I don't understand English. My language is Greek. The language I can understand. The language my *yiayia* – my grandmother – speaks to me. But this teacher, she spoke to me in English, leaning over me, and I couldn't understand her. So I put my hands

(Continued)

(Continued)

over my ears and screamed. My mum spoke to the teacher, then said good-bye to me, in Greek, and said she would come back later. Then she left.

The teacher took my hand and led me into the corner. She crouched down and spoke to me. Slowly. Right into my face. I didn't understand the words, but she sounded cross. I wanted my mum. I wanted my *yiayai*. I put my hands over my ears and screamed again, only louder, so I would not hear the words that I couldn't understand. I started to say some words in Greek. The teacher tried to take my hands from over my ears. I looked at her hand, pulling mine. I didn't like it so I bit it. This is how I started my first day at nursery school.

Maria is Greek, and she came to England in order to work and study English, just for a couple of years, or at least, that was the plan. She met an English man, and they married, bought a house, settled down and had Alex. Unfortunately, the marriage did not last. Maria's husband left when Alex was a baby and now has no contact with him. When Maria walked into the Home-Start office, she was struggling with bringing up Alex, now aged three. This is how she described their situation:

Maria: I am a single mum and Alex has experienced a number of changes in his life over the past three–four years. In 2006, I separated from Alex's father and Alex does not have any contact with him. We have lived at various houses in England and in Greece, before moving to our permanent address here. We returned to Greece for five months last year and Alex attended nursery there. Unfortunately, the nursery could not handle his behaviour and I felt it was best to return to the UK.

Since the marriage break-up, Maria had tried going back to live in her small village in Greece, surrounded and supported by her extended family, but that also had its difficulties. She felt she had moved on from her home culture, and she craved the life and independence she had experienced in England. Over the next two years, she travelled backwards and forwards between the two countries and two very different lifestyles, before deciding to settle permanently in England, and putting Alex into nursery.

By this time, Alex had forgotten English and now only understood Greek. He had left behind a large, supportive, extended family to come back to a small house with only his mother. He started a new nursery in England and found himself in unfamiliar surroundings, with teachers and children speaking a language he could not understand. This was yet one more frustrating and bewildering transition and probably explained why Alex's behaviour continued to deteriorate, and he used verbal and physical aggression in an attempt to express his feelings. Maria, as an adult, could intellectualise and discuss her situation and difficult feelings, whereas Alex, as a young child, was struggling to understand and make sense of all the changes in his life. This last transition has been extremely difficult for both Alex and Maria.

Maria (feeling isolated, unsupported, judged as a single mother and bad parent) said: 'Alex's behaviour at home is very challenging. He regularly hits me and displays aggression. He seems to have difficulty controlling his temper and becomes tearful and angry for no apparent reason. The nursery in Greece and his teacher here have raised concerns about his behaviour – his aggression towards teachers and other children, lack of concentration, difficulty following instructions and now instances of trying to take equipment home from school without her knowledge.'

Alex repeatedly told his mother that the other children at nursery called him 'the naughty boy'. In order to help Alex, the Home-Start co-ordinator recognised that Maria needed help by making her feel listened to and supported. Home-Start believes that children need a happy and secure childhood and that parents play the key role in giving their children a good start in life and helping them to achieve their full potential (see www.home-start.org.uk).

Three years after her marriage break-up, Maria was still struggling with the transition from, in her own words, 'middle class, respectable, secure, married mum, with a much wanted baby, living in our own home, with a part-time job' to a 'judged, foreign, single parent living on benefits in social housing, with a child with challenging behaviour'.

Maria's feelings were caused by her own response to transitions in her self-identity that were occurring as a result of all of the changes in her life: 'it's not the events, but rather the inner re-orientation and self redefinition that you have to go through in order to incorporate any of these changes into your life' (Bridges, 2004: xii).

The cumulative effects of the events in Alex's life, over which he had no control, were impacting on his transition to nursery. The effect on children of the parents' divorce and separation has been the subject of much research and writing. Pedro-Carroll writes: 'Parental divorce entails a series of transitions and family reorganisations that influence children's adjustment over time, including changes in residence, family relationships and standard of living' (Pedro-Carroll, 2005: 2). This was certainly the case for Alex. Pedro-Carroll goes on to quote studies by Hetherington et al. (1998) and Amato and Keith (1991), which show that, 'on average, children of divorced parents are less socially, emotionally and academically well adjusted than their peers in non divorced families' (Pedro-Carroll, 2005: 3). Maria was very anxious about the effects the divorce and separation

(Continued)

(Continued)

were having on Alex, particularly as his father played no part in his life. Her concerns are well recognised: 'the emotional repercussions of a parental separation can significantly affect the course of children's social and intellectual development' (Palmer, 2006: 149). It was apparent that Alex was having huge problems with this latest transition. Factors that might make transition harder include 'being the youngest in the group, speaking English as a second language or being a boy' (O'Connor, 2007: 3). Alex was disadvantaged by two of these three factors, but fortunately he had a persistent mother in Maria, who was determined to get help and support for herself and her unhappy son. Maria had asked about being matched with a male volunteer to give Alex a positive male role model. Home-Start had such a person available, Jim, who was a volunteer and a father of two boys with special needs.

Home-Start co-ordinator: I have been able to match Jim to this family – to be a good male role model for Alex, to play with him, help him practise his English, take him out, give his mum a break, listen to his mum, helping her to cope with her situation. By meeting the mother's needs, we help to enable her to cope and therefore meet the needs of her son.

Later that month Jim began visiting Maria and Alex on a weekly basis. He spent some time talking with and listening to Maria and then time with Alex, talking and playing with him. Often they would go out to the park or to a book shop, one of Alex's favourite places, to give Maria some time to herself.

After four weeks of visiting the family, Jim told his manager in supervision that Maria was tired and stressed and still finding Alex's behaviour and aggression towards her very difficult. Jim observed that a lot of Alex's behaviour appeared to be a result of frustration at not being able to express himself in English. Maria and Alex spoke Greek at home (at Alex's behest). Jim's two to three hours a week, one to one, speaking English became an important part of the case work. Only four weeks from the start of his involvement Jim could see Alex's English improving. Jim also reported that Maria was happy that Alex was now 'in the system' after the GP made a referral to a paediatrician for an assessment of Alex's behaviour and development.

At this point Maria told Home-Start of a significant decision she had made. A few months earlier, feeling isolated and alone, she had returned to her family in Greece at every opportunity:

Maria: We spent the summer in Greece with my family, where everyone looked after Alex – he had loads of attention, and I could relax and have some time for myself. But back home in England, it's just me and Alex,

24 hours a day – no dad – no extended family. Alex reacted badly to coming back – he is angry, and bored, attention seeking and difficult.

Now that she was now feeling more supported, Maria had decided, for Alex's sake, not to return to Greece for the Christmas break. She told Jim that it would be very hard to be apart from her family, but she felt that Alex would benefit. Every time they returned to Greece, Alex thought they had gone 'home'; he loved being with the extended family, he would forget all his English, and he would be upset and even more difficult to cope with on their return. By staying, she could help him practise his English, spend some positive time with him and help him to think of their house as his permanent home. This was a very courageous decision for Maria to make, and one that would really benefit Alex while he was still trying to settle into nursery, and accept England and their house as 'home'. This was an example of a positive outcome because Maria was beginning to have her own needs met (i.e. some understanding and support) thus enabling her to meet her child's needs.

Maria was constantly being told about Alex's 'bad' behaviour in feedback from the nursery. To counter this negativity, Jim was careful to give Maria positive feedback after any outing with Alex. He would tell her when he had been good, how he enjoyed their outings and how much fun Alex could be. This had a positive effect on Maria's mood and self-esteem and Maria also admitted she was now enjoying Alex more.

After Christmas Alex settled back into nursery a little better, but Maria began worrying that Alex was unlikely to get a place at the school attached to his nursery as it was very oversubscribed. She was concerned that a change to another school would be another painful transition which would adversely affect Alex. Jim told Maria that parents could request a place in a certain school in special circumstances such as social, educational or health reasons. Maria had not been aware of this. Her written English was not good and she was anxious her application would fail. She asked Jim to help her write her letter and the manager also wrote a letter of support from Home-Start. She suggested that Maria ask her GP to do the same. Once again, because she felt supported and cared for, Maria felt strong enough not to go back to her family in Greece for Easter but stay at home.

This time, when he returned to the nursery in April, Alex was happier and settled in very quickly. His English was greatly improved: now he could communicate with the teachers and his peers. One day he even got a badge from the nursery as a reward for good behaviour. One morning in April, the Home-Start manager received a phone call from Maria who was ecstatic:

(Continued)

(Continued)

Maria: Thank you so much, Alex has a place in the school for September, he can stay where he is, and it's one transition he won't have to cope with.

Alex: Wednesday mornings, that's when my special friend, Jim, comes to see me. Sometimes Jim talks to my mum for a bit, then he plays with me. Sometimes we make things, or he reads to me, or we talk and play with my toys. Most weeks he takes me out somewhere – to the park, or in his car to an indoor play park or to the bookshop.

Jim is my special friend. I say to him. 'I like you Jim, you are my special friend', and he said he likes me too. I said, 'Thank you Jim for liking me'. I think my daddy didn't like me. He didn't love me. But my mummy says everyone loves me and she loves me. Sometimes when I am cross I say I will go back to Greece to live and she can go and live with my daddy. Or I tell her to go and I will find my daddy and live with him.

But on our last holiday we didn't go back there, and it was just me and my mum in our house and I missed everyone. I didn't go to nursery and Jim didn't come, but me and my mum went for walks and played in the snow, and it was just us and my mum didn't cry. I used to cry every day at nursery. But now I don't. My mummy comes to fetch me and she says, 'Did you cry today?' and I say, 'No!' She says, 'Did you sit on the time-out chair?' and I say. 'Yes!' She asks me why and I say it is because I didn't sit still on the carpet, or I talked when I shouldn't, but she doesn't get cross.

It's better now I can understand what people are saying to me more. I can talk to the other children and they understand me, and now I like nursery. I can talk to Jim and he can understand me and we talk.

This week Mummy had a letter and it said I could stay at the same school in September when I go to big school. My mummy said she wrote and asked them if I could stay because it is the same school with the same friends, and I am happy I can stay.

The Home-Start manager visited Maria at the end of April, in order to review Home-Start's support. She was not the tearful, depressed mother that she had been some months ago. Now she was smiling, relaxed and happy.

Home-Start manager: I found Maria pottering at home. She made us coffee and we sat down to talk. She has had Alex's place at the school confirmed. She is so grateful for Home-Start's help in getting the place, and suggesting that her GP could also write a letter. She was smiling and saying she is happy – no comparison with a year ago! Alex is happier – now he enjoys nursery where he used to hate it. Now he says, 'I didn't cry today, Mummy' and 'I had fun today'.

In a reflective supervision session, Jim commented, 'This is what I signed up for; it's what volunteering is all about'. Seeing the positive changes in Maria and Alex over the last eight months has made this a satisfying piece of work for him.

Dilemmas for the Home-Start manager

Relationships matter

There are many reasons why Home-Start support works. First, it is accessible. Like Maria, many families simply contact them directly, and a Home-Start co-ordinator visits them to discuss their needs. Second, bureaucracy is minimal; within a month of meeting Maria and listening to her story, a volunteer had been found who began visiting her in her own home for three hours a week in order to meet her need for practical and emotional support. Families are empowered by Home-Start. It is their choice to have the service, no matter who refers them, and they can end the support at any time.

The relationship between the volunteer and the supported parent is key, but while there needs to be a building of friendship and trust, this must be 'boundaried' and supervised, so that the volunteer does not become over involved, and the parent does not become too dependent on the volunteer. In order to safeguard against this, regular review visits to the family and supervision for the volunteer are vital components of the work.

Preparing for the end of the transition support

The moment Home-Start begins working with a family, it is not only attempting to meet the family's needs, but already working towards the next transition: the time when the family will not need Home-Start support any more.

At Home-Start the volunteer provides a supported relationship within agreed boundaries; a relationship which must come to an end, and which must be prepared for. It was important that as well as feeling empowered by inviting Home-Start into their lives, Maria and Alex must be part of the planning for the ending – a transition which could feel positive and owned, rather than thrust upon them. The ending should always be discussed, prepared for, and owned by all parties – the family and the volunteer.

The strength of being outside the government's agenda

Home-Start's focus on working with the parents in order to help the children is very much a feature of the government 'Think Family' agenda.

> DCSF are developing cross-government guidance and protocols to support and reinforce the local implementation of the Think Family approach to delivering services. These guidance and protocols call for adults and children's services and health and voluntary sector partners to work more closely together and take a whole family approach to secure better outcomes for children from families with complex needs. (DCSF.gov.uk/everychildmatters)

The 'Think Family' agenda describes the way Home-Start has been working for almost 40 years. But very often national or local policy may suddenly demand a different way of working, or dictate new outcomes. There is the constant challenge, the uncomfortable balancing of remaining true to the Home-Start ethos, to do what works in terms of how we support families, and has worked since its inception in 1973, while meeting the changing priorities of funders, local and national agendas.

Home-Start is part of the voluntary sector. Because it is seen as completely separate from the statutory sector, 'hard-to-reach families' that are so often mentioned in statutory targets will engage with it. The separateness builds a relationship of trust and opens the door for Home-Start to help. Families that are suspicious of social services will often accept a Home-Start volunteer. How can Home-Start keep this 'difference' when government agendas increasingly want it to become indistinguishable from other statutory agencies?

The Home-Start manager's perspectives

This case study shows that situations are not hopeless: 'The ability [to cope with change] is likely to be rooted in our childhood experiences, as the children who are supported through early transitions learn positive ways of coping ... at any stage of their lives' (O'Connor, 2007: 1). Children are very resilient, and by working together to help them through difficult times, situations can be turned around. When Home-Start began working with this family no-one had any idea what the outcome would be. Home-Start's vision is that with the support of a caring, non-judgemental volunteer, who has the time to build up a relationship with this family, there is the potential for positive change.

The GP had referred Alex for a paediatric assessment, in case his challenging behaviour had a medical reason: perhaps he suffered from Asperger's syndrome or was on the autistic spectrum. The staff at the nursery school seemed to view Alex as naughty, and Maria was left feeling that this was her fault, and did not feel supported or understood by the school. They suggested that she attended a parenting programme.

Home-Start manager: My efforts to engage in a dialogue with the paediatrician and with the school in order to help Alex were rebuffed. The paediatrician did not answer my letter, and although the nursery allowed me to visit the class, the nursery workers were defensive and uninterested in my role. The teacher simply wanted to point out any incidents where Alex was 'difficult' or 'naughty'. I had hoped to share good practice, and to perhaps explore whether Alex's difficult behaviour, aggression, lack of concentration, etc. was because he had a condition such as ADHD or autism, or was actually as a result of the difficult transitions of the last three years.

Jo-anne Pedro-Carroll argues:

> Children can develop areas of resilience in their lives when they are protected by the positive actions of adults, by good nurturing, by their assets and by policies and practices that support their healthy development and reduce risk across key systems (legal, judicial, educational, family, community) that affect their lives. (2005: 4)

Having spent time with Maria, and learning about her life, I felt confident that with the right support, she and Alex would start to adjust to their situation. I hoped that there were enough positive actions of adults in Alex's life, and Maria's, to help make a positive difference.

Stop Press! Update on the case study

Maria and Alex have just left to go to Greece, their first visit in a year, to go 'on holiday' rather than 'go back home'. Alex is due to start full-time school, and has been discharged by the paediatrician. Maria is at college doing an IT course, and is a parent representative on the board of her local children's centre. She plans to train as a Home-Start volunteer next year.

📖 Further Reading

Bridges, W. (2004) *Transitions – Making Sense of Life's Changes*, 2nd edn. Cambridge, MA: Da Capo Press.

This book deals with the transitions in an individual's life – marriages and divorces, family births and deaths, relocations and career changes, retirement and all the other personal changes that can disrupt our lives.

Palmer, S. (2006) *Toxic Childhood*. London: Orion.

This book explains how a toxic mix of side-effects of cultural change is affecting the development of a growing number of children. It also explains how a few simple adjustments to lifestyle can 'detoxify' children's lives.

Sinclair, A (2007) *0–5: How Small Children Make a Big Difference*. London: The Work Foundation Report. Provocation Series, Vol. 3, No. 1.

This excellent and thought-provoking report argues for renewed investment in the early lives of children, for the benefit of society as a whole. The paper demonstrates how vital the early years are to good economics, social mobility, quality of life and, consequently, government plans for modernisation and reform.

11

From neglected to protected

Mariana Graham

Chapter Overview

This chapter looks at a short, but life-changing period in the life of Aaron and his family. A case study describes Aaron's journey from living in a loving but neglectful home, where his mother is unable to meet all his emotional and developmental needs, to one where he and his family are supported by professionals to ensure that his mother is enabled to provide good care for Aaron and his siblings. The case study and discussion is told from the point of view of a child-protection conference chair. A child-protection conference is a meeting that brings together the family members, the child (where appropriate) and professionals involved with the child and family. Child-protection conferences aim to collect and analyse information about the child and his or her circumstances; to consider the evidence presented as well as the historical information; to make judgements as to whether the child is suffering significant harm or likely to suffer significant harm; and to decide what future action is required to prevent further harm. This chapter also explains how the child-protection conference can be used as a vehicle for change and support during periods of transition. Aaron's journey exemplifies change and support brought about by the professionals and family working together.

Introduction to the case study

The Adams family is composed of Ms Adams, Aaron (aged six), Sophie and Sarah (aged three), Connor (aged one) and Mary (aged ten, living with her father). Only two previous referrals have been received by children services prior to the incident that resulted in the child-protection conferences for the children. Several years ago concerns were raised about the care provided to Mary by Ms Adams and poor home conditions. This resulted in Mary moving to live with her paternal family from the aged of nine months. Three years ago it was alleged that the children were left on their own with a 12-year-old babysitter. No further action was taken when the police attended and found that a 16-year-old, his sister and a friend were looking after the children.

 Unable to care for the children?

Soon after Aaron started reception he was the subject of a CAF (Common Assessment Framework) with regular TAF (Team Around the Child) meetings held by the school. Ms Adams initially engaged with all the services and support offered by the school and the local children's centre, but did not maintain her engagement. Sophie and Sarah's school attendance were poor, although it was acknowledged that they were not yet of compulsory school-going age. The children's clothes were dirty and their appearance raised concerns. The school provided Aaron with extra clothes as his were not clean. Sophie and Sarah often appeared to be hungry and smelled of urine. Aaron's behaviour was described as 'challenging at times' and he was finding it increasingly difficult to adhere to boundaries within the classroom.

The children missed various medical appointments. Aaron missed an appointment for a paediatric assessment to establish whether his behaviour could be attributed to ADHD (attention deficit hyperactive disorder). He also missed appointments for vision testing and testing for dyslexia. Sophie and Sarah were not toilet trained. Sophie and Sarah were referred to a speech therapist as their speech and comprehension were delayed. The health visitor was concerned that Sophie and Sarah were under-stimulated. No concerns were raised about Connor's health or development. He was described as a placid child.

Ms Adams did not have a close relationship with her brother or mother. She had some friends, but they were not reliable and she was in fact very isolated. Ms Adams made it clear that nobody knew that she was not coping. Ms Adams described feeling as if she was in a big hole that she could not get out of and that she did not know what to do. Ms Adams always suffered with depression. She found out that the children's father had another family that she did not know about. Ms Adams admitted to alcohol and drug misuse in the past and told professionals that she stopped using alcohol about two years ago and drugs about six years ago.

One Saturday at 4.14 a.m. a neighbour found Aaron and his sister Sophie on a pavement outside. They called the police. Aaron and Sophie were found to be dehydrated and they smelled strongly of ammonia (urine). Aaron and Sophie were taken into police protection whilst they made further enquiries to find their parent and home. When located, Ms Adams was unaware that the children were not in the house. Ms Adams assumed that the children slipped through the front door while she was asleep on the sofa. The home conditions were extremely poor and smelled strongly of faeces and urine. There was no adequate bedding for the children. There was rubbish and dirty nappies all over the house. There were no clean clothes for the children. There was some food in the freezer. Sarah and Connor were also taken into police protection and Ms Adams was arrested on suspicion of neglect.

Ms Adams admitted the charges against her when interviewed by the police. She told the officers that she was struggling to cope and was depressed. She found Aaron's behaviour difficult to manage and thought he might have ADHD. It was evident that Ms Adams loved her children dearly. Ms Adams was cautioned for child neglect and no further action was taken by the police. They were of the view that Ms Adams was genuinely remorseful and that her circumstances and depression had a significant impact on her parenting.

The children were placed in foster care (with agency foster carers) as there were no family or friends that could care for them. Sarah and Sophie were placed together whilst Aaron and Connor were placed together. The first placement for Aaron and Connor was an emergency placement only and the children had to move to a second placement further away from home on the Monday. Due to the foster carers' own anxieties and concerns about their ability to manage Aaron's behaviour, he and Connor were moved to a third placement. Again this foster placement found it difficult to manage Aaron's behaviour. He was described as being aggressive, challenging, having violent rages and threatening to throw himself down the stairs. Connor stayed in this placement and Aaron moved to his fourth foster placement. Within one day this carer also asked for Aaron to be moved. This is a total of four foster placements in 16 days.

Working together for the children

Aaron had his fifth move when he returned to the care of Ms Adams. After a few months all the children returned home. At that time Ms Adams made

(Continued)

(Continued)

some significant efforts to clean and clear the house of all rubbish and also did some decorating with the help of family and friends.

As a result of the removal of the children the service provision with the family changed from a CAF, to children looked after (CLA) to child protection (CP). The initial child-protection conference took place before the children returned to the care of Ms Adams. Aaron, Sophie, Sarah and Connor were all made subjects to child-protection plans in the category of neglect. The initial plan identified the need for a detailed and in-depth parenting assessment, support for the children and Ms Adams, the importance of the children being seen for their health appointments and a referral to the community paediatrician for a full developmental and health assessment of Aaron. The plan also contained specific points to support Ms Adams as well as the children with their education, health and overall development. It also included a contingency plan should there be any further concerns about the care being provided to the children.

During the next two review child-protection conferences many positive changes were highlighted. The children have all remained in the care of Ms Adams and she continued to engage with the child-protection plan and all professionals involved.

At the time of the third review child-protection conference, almost a year later, a third social worker was working with the family. The school nurse (for Aaron, Sophie and Sarah), health visitor (for Connor), school (for Aaron, Sophie and Sarah), behavioural support team (for Aaron), specialist children's team (Ms Adams), nursery nurse (Ms Adams) and two community paediatricians (Aaron and Sarah) were involved with the family.

Ms Adams initially sought help for her depression from her GP, but continued to have some very low days when she still struggled to provide for the basic care needs of the children. She stopped taking medication for depression and chose not to engage with any counselling or support for herself. Aaron was diagnosed with segmental neurofibromatosis, type NF1. This condition can be associated with learning disability and behavioural difficulties. This implied that Aaron's learning and behavioural difficulties are not necessarily only as a result of his needs being neglected. However there is also a history of learning difficulties in Aaron's family and the community paediatrician also explained to Ms Adams that poor routines, poor boundaries and neglect will have a definite impact and could lead to increased behavioural difficulties. Aaron was prescribed medication to help and reduce his disturbed sleeping patterns. Sarah was receiving treatment for a small bladder, which could be contributing to the difficulty she has in being toilet trained.

The nursery nurse and worker from the specialist children's team were providing ongoing support and guidance to Ms Adams on improving boundaries, routines and stimulation for the children as well as working on maintaining an adequate family home. Information also came to light that Ms Adams found it difficult to learn at school and might have a learning disability. This could have a direct impact on her understanding of the concerns, her ability to maintain changes and therefore on her parenting.

However, at this time all the professionals expressed their concerns that Ms Adams would struggle to maintain an adequate level of care should the professional support be withdrawn. It was feared that she would not be able to make the necessary health appointments, or attend them, without the intensive support provided by the school nurse. The concern also remained that Ms Adams was not receiving treatment for her depression; she continued to be very isolated and without a reliable support network. The risk therefore remained that Ms Adams would not be able to maintain an acceptable standard of care and that the children would suffer chronic neglect. The children continued to be subject to protection plans in the category of neglect and recommendations were made that a specialist parenting assessment of Ms Adams should be undertaken to assess her ability to make the changes and provide good enough care to her children.

Dilemmas for the social worker

Smith et al. (1998) highlight that the effects of abuse (including neglect) can be wide ranging and long lasting, but more importantly they identify that there are factors that can decrease the impact on the child. These factors include the coping strategies used by the child, the support they have and their ability to understand and appreciate what has happened to them. Joint working between the family and multi-agencies is one of the main forms of support that children involved with the child-protection process will have. The process of joint working can clearly be found in the child-protection conference process. The specific needs of the children in the Adams family, the services and support offered by the multi-agency network of professionals and the possible outcomes for the children are portrayed in the case study. All the dimensions of the child's life are closely linked together but also the needs of the child, the service providers involved and the possible outcomes are all linked too.

The following diagram may be used to bring the focus back to the child, the professionals and processes needed to support children in transitions.

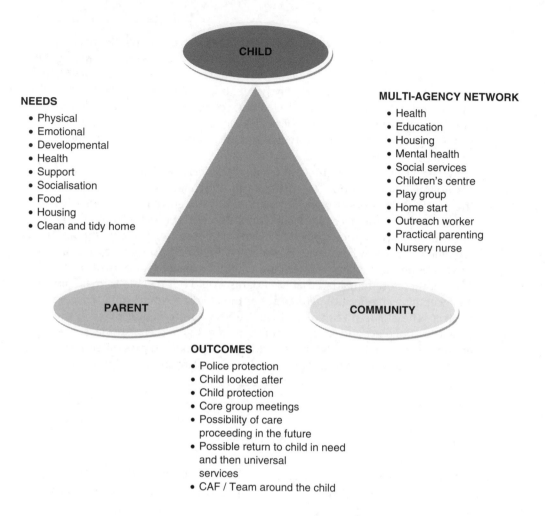

NEEDS
- Physical
- Emotional
- Developmental
- Health
- Support
- Socialisation
- Food
- Housing
- Clean and tidy home

MULTI-AGENCY NETWORK
- Health
- Education
- Housing
- Mental health
- Social services
- Children's centre
- Play group
- Home start
- Outreach worker
- Practical parenting
- Nursery nurse

OUTCOMES
- Police protection
- Child looked after
- Child protection
- Core group meetings
- Possibility of care proceeding in the future
- Possible return to child in need and then universal services
- CAF / Team around the child

An appreciative inquiry approach

Integrated practice and multi-agency working to safeguard children have changed significantly in the past ten years. Although these changes were much needed at the given period it is concerning that there has not been any really significant change in how we manage the child-protection conference process. This can often be found to be punitive and intrusive for families as well as professionals and has not always been seen as the most effective way of achieving change and outcomes for children.

It is encouraging to note that there is movement to change the conference process with more local authorities changing to or considering adapting the conference structure towards what is known in the UK as the Strengthening Families Model for child-protection conferences.

The Strengthening Families Model is based on the Signs of Safety Approach that was first used in Australia. Dr Andrew Turnell (2010: 36) closely links this approach, and therefore the Strengthening Families Model, to an Appreciative Inquiry used within child protection. He described the use of this model as supporting practitioners, external agencies and families to work towards a culture of reflection and increasing practice depth, which will ultimately support and achieve better outcomes for children.

Before looking further at the meaning of this in practice, it is important to remind ourselves what an Appreciative Inquiry is and what the most common practice has been in recent years. The experiences of social workers, managers and conference chairs, are that child-protection conferences are rarely seen as positive events. Families, as well as some professionals, can find them extremely stressful and difficult to understand and deal with. The most commonly used conference process could be describe as a critical incident as well as a period of transition for most children, parents or carers and even for professionals. A tendency has developed in the social work profession to identify what has gone wrong and what needs to change known as the critical incident inquiry. Kain describes the critical incident technique as follows:

> The critical incident technique essentially involves asking a number of respondents to identify events or experiences that were 'critical' for some purpose. These incidents are then pooled together for analysis, and generalizations about the event or activity are drawn from the commonalities of the incidents. (Kain, 2004: 71)

He argues that using the critical incident technique relies heavily on the significance others place on the events. Using the critical incident technique as an aid to learning is not always productive or even a positive experience. It creates a culture of 'lessons learned' without any real vision as to what could be done to improve outcomes for children. Kolb further highlights the risks in using the critical incident approach by differentiating between appreciation and critical comprehension: 'appreciation is an act of attention, valuing and affirmation, whereas critical comprehension is based on objectivity, dispassionate analysis and scepticism' (Kolb in Cooperrider and Srivastva, 1987: 28). A key difference from critical incident inquiry is that an Appreciative Inquiry identifies what is working or has worked well and then looks at what can be done to make things even better. Cooperrider and Srivastva (1987: 25) identify four principles of Appreciative Inquiry. In summary they are:

1 To begin with there should be appreciation and acknowledgement that every system works to some degree.

2 The process and outcome should be applicable with knowledge that can be used, applied and put into action.

3 It should recognise that the system is more capable and able to learn how to take part.

4 It is a collaborative process where there is a relationship between the process of the inquiry and its content.

The Signs of Safety Approach (Turnell, 2010) uses the same approach and can be used across a multi-agency network.

Applying appreciative inquiry to this case study

A Strengthening Families Model approach focuses on the specific key areas of current risk, historical/complicating factors, grey areas, positives/strengths and protective factors whilst at the same time using the 4-D cycle of Appreciative Inquiry, as explained by Ricciardi (2004). The case study of the Adams family can be used to explain the processes in more detail.

Discovery: appreciation of what is

The main aim and focus of any child-protection conference is to hear information from families and professionals to identify what the current circumstances are for the child. This will also include any relevant historical information. This is not always an easy task as cases mainly come to conference because of things that have gone wrong.

Ms Adams dearly loves her children and they had a significant bond with their mother. Ms Adams has been able to provide some good parenting as the children did not previously come to the attention of social services. The onset of Ms Adams's depression raised concerns with professionals and support was put in place; unfortunately, this did not succeed, as Ms Adams did not engage. Another positive was the fact that Ms Adams accepted full responsibility for her actions acknowledging, rather than blaming, the impact her depression and circumstances have on her parenting ability.

Dream: what might be

Although this would appear to be an easy and straightforward process, this could be flawed if it is not made specific to each child's circumstances. It would be very easy to *assume* in this phase what life should be like for the child and family. However, this is the perfect opportunity to listen to the child and family and hear what their dreams for the future are. A recent study into the views of children by D'Cruz and Stagnitti (2010) emphasised the importance of professionals working with families and children asking the views of children about their perception of being loved and cared for as a means to inform professional judgements to intervene.

The 'dream' that Ms Adams and her children had was to be able to live together as a family. Aaron was able to express this view to the social worker. Ms Adams does not want to suffer with depression. Ms Adams would like to receive support to manage Aaron's sometimes difficult behaviour and the toilet training for Sophie and Sarah. The professionals involved with this family also have their 'dreams': first, to ensure that the children remain in the care of Ms Adams unless it is deemed to place them in harm's way and, second, to ensure that Ms Adams and the children are offered support to make the changes they need.

Design: what should be

The design phase of the conference identifies what change is needed in order to ensure that the child protection plans are safe to be discontinued and in some cases to prevent further, more extreme interventions of initiating care proceedings. This will focus on the changes that the parent/carer need to make in order to ensure that risk of harm to the child is reduced. In certain cases, this could also relate to the expectations of the child/young person and the changes they have to make to reduce the risk they place themselves in. This phase should focus on all aspects of the child's development and circumstances, including health, education, emotional well-being, family and social relationships and environmental factors.

The concerns held by professionals for the Adams' family are clear, specific and detailed, and it is therefore easy to identify what should be different for the children:

- Aaron and Ms Adams need support to understand and manage his behavioural difficulties.

- The house needs to be a safe environment for the children.

- Sophie and Sarah need to be toilet trained.

- The children should not be left unsupervised.

- There need to be clear routines and boundaries in place for all four of the children.

- Ms Adams's mental health should not impact on her parenting ability.

- All the health needs of the children should be provided for.

Delivery: creating what will be

The process of gathering the information and ultimately the creation of the protection plan is the delivery phase of the conference. The protection plan provides an outline of assessments, support and services to be put in place for the adults and children. The plan further identifies who will be responsible for certain tasks and provide a clear timescale for implementation. The protection plan should be specific, measurable, achievable, realistic and with clear timescales identified to ensure that there is no drift or delay for children. If it is not, you are likely to set up to fail not only the family, but also the professionals linked to the case. Most of all, the plan should include not only the needs identified in the design phase, but also those of the dream phase. The plan is then reviewed at regular core group meetings (smaller meetings with the professionals and family) to ensure that circumstances are reviewed and the plan progressed. An example of such a plan is:

- Aaron should be seen by the community paediatrician for a full assessment of his development and health on a specific date.

- Aaron should continue to attend the Nurture Group at school weekly to help him make friends at school and talk about his feelings in a safe place at school.

- Health visitor should continue to have contact with Ms Adams at least once every two weeks to support Ms Adams with advice and strategies on toilet training for Sophie and Sarah.

- Ms Adams should continue to take medication for her depression and to attend any counselling appointments offered to her to help her overcome her past experiences and receive support for her own mental health difficulties.

Taking note of the child's views

Most importantly the need remains for the family and professionals to 'hear the voice of the child' throughout the child protection and conference process to ensure that all planning and actions are meaningful. Articles 12 and 13 of The Convention on the Rights of Children (UNICEF, 2009: 10) requires that children have a right to say what they think should happen to them, to have their opinions taken into account (Article 12) and they have a right to share information (Article 13).

Ensuring that children have a voice also impacts on their own resilience. Resilience or ability to cope and deal with circumstances in life plays a significant role in lessening the risk and impact of negative experiences for children. Gilligan (2010: 178) states that supportive relationships are a requirement for resilience in children. Newman and Blackburn (2002) suggest that a sense of mastery and belief that one's own efforts can make a difference and their ability or opportunity to 'make a difference' also contribute to resilience building in children.

The impact of love and support

A former head teacher, Lynn Cousins (2007), shared her experiences and views of the impact factors contributing to resilience can have on transitions. She found that a child who faces transition with love and support would view change in a more positive light than the child who has been harshly criticised, punished or ridiculed at these times. The child who was supported will learn to deal confidently with transition, while the other child will be afraid of facing new challenges. Turnbull (2006: 5) argues that unsuccessful transitions could have negative implications for the future well-being of a child and their capacity to enjoy and achieve in their childhood and adolescence. This is especially true for children in neglectful and abusive families. It is fair to say that it should not be assumed that children will not or could not respond to difficult situations (Gilligan, 2010: 177), but we should still strive towards providing children with the opportunities and support to build their resilience, which will have a direct impact on their ability to manage transitions in life.

Attachment theorists have identified the importance of the child-hood experiences on later life. Hinde and Stevenson-Hinde linked the influence and importance of childhood experiences on later life:

> the only predictor of later environments available to the young individual is the current environment ... young individuals ... use the quality of their early environment as an index of what life would be like when they grew up, and to develop personalities suitable for such an 'anticipated' environment. (1991: 57)

The Child Protection Chair's Perspective

My main role when chairing child protection conferences is to ensure that all the relevant information is shared and reviewed. This helps to ensure that the correct decision and recommendations are made. In this process it is important to ensure that the family as well as professionals are able to be comfortable and at ease during the meeting to support and allow them to 'tell their story'. I have since learned that the best way to do this is to ask the family and professionals firstly what they are worried about, secondly what they think the positives and strengths are and thirdly to identify what needs to be put into place to remove and change what they are worried about.

Most of all the focus has to be on what the outcome for the child or children in this family will be and to ensure that I support and enable all involved to ensure that change is achieved for the child.

Reflections

The main role of being a conference chair is to be an interprofessional leader. There can be a multitude of different professions and indeed professionals around one table and each one of them will bring a wealth of experience and significant information about the family. Chairing a conference is a constant learning process and there is not one recipe for how to do it. One of the most important lessons I have learnt is that the starting point should always be to ensure that everybody at a conference, especially the family and child, is able to a part of the bigger picture to ensure that change is brought about for the child.

Stop Press! Update on the case study

Unfortunately for Aaron and his siblings Ms Adams found it very difficult to maintain the changes she made when professionals started to withdraw their support to allow her to start and take some responsibility. Ms Adams continued to struggle with her own mental health. The last information I have about this family was that children's services were planning to issue care proceedings to ensure that the right decisions are made about the future care arrangements for the children. As I am no longer working for the local authority responsible for the Adams family, I do not have an update on the current circumstances of the children.

Further Reading

Horwarth, J. (ed.) *The Child's World: The Comprehensive Guide to Assessing Children in Need*, 2nd edn. London: Jessica Kingsley Publishers.

This book contains a vast amount of information and references for any professional working with children and their families. It provides a good starting point to understand what is meant by assessment and how to distinguish between the different levels of need and risk.

Munro, E. (2011) *The Munro Review of Child Protection: Final Report – A Child Centred Analysis.* www.education.gov.uk/publications/eOrderingDownload/Cm%208062.pdf (accessed 7 November 2011).

Professor Eileen Munro carried out a comprehensive review of child protection and practice. This is the final report and contains the recommendations she made to ensure that any work with children and families focuses on their needs so that they have the best outcomes in life.

Turnell, A. (2010) The signs of safety: a comprehensive briefing paper. www.scie-socialcareonline.org.uk/profile.asp?guid=78c4826a-8b52-4b6d-bd7a-5ec28f98ec6e (accessed 7 November 2011).

This paper provides significant information about the new Strengthening Families Model that is being introduced by local authorities to use for child protection conferences all over the country. It outlines the reasons behind this model, and explains its purpose and focus.

12

Experiencing the death of a parent

Pamela Curran

Chapter Overview

The death of a parent can be one of the most traumatic transitions that a child encounters and the effect of this significant change in a child's life can have devastating and long-term consequences. For the child, and any surviving parent, this life-altering event can bring confusion, disruption and anguish. This chapter will explore some of the experiences expressed following the sudden and unexpected death of a parent. It aims to show how 'listening to the voice of the child' can improve the support offered at this difficult time. The chapter is written by a health visitor. Health visitors are trained nurses who have received additional specialist training in public health and are trained to assess, support and work with families in identifying potential concerns along with promoting health and development. Through leadership and working in partnership with other agencies they initiate and promote the Healthy Child Programme (DoH, 2009b). This role includes the assessment and support of families during various transitions in their lives and aims to ensure that children have a positive start, thereby laying the foundations for their future well-being and health (DoH, 2007, 2011).

No official numbers of bereaved children are currently recorded; however it is estimated that between 4 and 7 per cent of 16-year-olds have been bereaved of a parent. The organisation Winston's Wish have estimated that 24,000 children are bereaved each year (Children's Bereavement Network, 2010; Winston's Wish, 2010). Historically a lack of research and statistical evidence has resulted in the specific needs of some of these children being unmet. There has been a long-standing misguided assumption that because a young child's cognitive development restricts their understanding of death (Wolfenstein, 1966) they therefore have a reduced need to be supported. More recent research however demonstrates that children do indeed express grief. This grief can be seen in a variety of behaviours including some non-verbal or difficult to recognise behaviours such as thumb sucking, bed wetting or tummy aches, even under the age of two years (Christ, 2000; Leeds Animation Workshop, 2005). These children can also have an increased risk of additional difficult events during their childhood including behaviour difficulties and school exclusion (Yagla Mack, 2001), lower levels of self-confidence and higher rates of depression thereby making them vulnerable to future health and social difficulties (National Children's Bureau, 2009). These children have a right to be supported through this transition to improve their well-being, long-term health and educational outcomes.

Introduction to case studies

The case studies illustrate the experiences of two children who had been suddenly and unexpected bereaved of a parent and they are presented from the child's perspective as the 'voice of a child'. With the first child, support had not yet been initiated, whereas with the second child strategies had been put in place to support the child and family.

 **Polly's story**

Polly was three years old at the time of her mother's death and went to live with her grandmother as a result. Polly demonstrated a state of confusion and distress but her attempts to give meaning to the situation were hampered by the fact that, at three years old, her cognitive maturity restricts her ability to fully comprehend the circumstances (Hatter, 1996). Developmentally she has not reached an age where she fully comprehends the finality of death; although her grandmother had frequently told her that her mother was in 'heaven' she still frequently asked and demanded to go 'home'.

(Continued)

(Continued)

Her limited ability to articulate her anxiety and grief in words results in her displaying more difficult to recognise signs of distress, such as her 'tummy hurts' or her 'legs were scratchy'. Her previously controlled ailments of asthma and eczema flared up and were harder to control. She also demonstrated long periods of time when she just sat in front of the TV whimpering or saying her 'crickle' hurt (a word she had made up). When asked what was the matter, she said she didn't know.

Polly: My name is Polly and I am 3 and ¾ years old. When I was at Nanny's flat a lady came to talk to Nanny. Nanny said that my Mummy had died. Nanny said that Mummy's body did not work anymore and she was in heaven. She said I would not be able to see her anymore. I had a big pain in my tummy. So I cried and cried and stamped my feet and shouted. Nanny gave me a big hug, but my tummy still hurt. Nanny said my mummy had gone to heaven and that she was now with Nanny's mummy in heaven. They were talking together in heaven. I don't want Mummy to be in heaven – I want her to come home and talk to me!

Nanny has made me a special room just for me at her flat. I have a pretty bed and a pink duvet. Pink is my favourite colour. But I don't like night time at Nanny's. At night time my tummy 'crickles'. It makes me wake up and it hurts. I go to see my Nanny and she puts me back to bed, but the 'crickle' is still there. I want to go home to my home and see Mummy!

At night my legs hurt and are scratchy. I want medicine, so Nanny gives me medicine with some water, and then gives me my cuddly toy to help my legs not hurt, but they still do! And the 'crickle' hurts too. I don't want the medicine or the water or my cuddly toy. I want to watch TV but Nanny said it was the middle of the night but I want to, I want to watch it *now*! I want Mummy, but Nanny said I couldn't. I don't like Nanny. I tell her 'I don't like you anymore. I like my Mummy. I want to go home, to my house, now.'

Nanny takes me to my nursery. I like going to my nursery. At nursery I like to play with the other children. We like to play monsters and running games. I like going to birthday parties because we have ice cream and chocolate. I have a big smiley face when I have ice cream and chocolate. Yum! Yum!

When Nanny picks me up, I ask to go home to Mummy, but she says 'no' I have to stay with her. I don't want to so I cry very loud. Nanny can sometimes get cross with me. When I come home from nursery I feel tired, Nanny says she has made me a special meal, but I don't like it, it doesn't taste the same as my Mummy's. Nanny can get cross when I don't eat but I don't want to. I am very tired, I want to go to sleep, I want to sleep on the sofa, I don't like my bedroom at Nanny's flat. Nanny gets cross and says how nice she has made my bedroom, a pink duvet and pretty bed but I want my bedroom at Mummy's flat.

Sometimes I feel strange and it makes my tummy hurt and my leg scratchy. I don't like it, so I scream and shout and cry. Nanny asked, 'What is the matter?', but I don't know.

 Matt's story

Matt's parents were separated and Matt was living with his mother when at the age of four his father died. His mother stated he had experienced periods of confusion and distress following the sudden death, which she expressed as 'he wanted to look after me' and 'be the man of the house' but was also 'in trouble' at school which culminated in him being excluded for a few days.

At the time of the study, it had been 18 months since the death and the family had moved to Hertfordshire. For Matt the bereavement had been distanced by time, he was also six years old and so significantly older developmentally than Polly, meaning that his progressing cognitive development was maturing his understanding of death (Beckett and Taylor, 2010).

Matt: My name is Matt and I am now six years old. I like playing football. I can run very fast and get the ball and score goals. Mummy said we can join a football team. I want to be the striker as I am very fast. I go to a big school but I am not always happy. My Mummy says that is OK.

When I was four I lived by the seaside with my Mummy and Daddy, but they got cross with each other and they decided not to live together, but I still saw my daddy lots and lots. Then my daddy had 'like a heart attack but in his head'. Mummy said he had died.

When we lived by the seaside I didn't like it, I went to school but didn't like it. I had a sad face on the inside then. Last summer, Mummy and I came here and I go to a different school. I like it better now. Mummy went to my new school and spoke to my new teacher Mrs T. Mrs T has told me that I can talk to her about anything or anyone, I can as many times as I like. But I don't always want to.

My mum and I went to special club. It's for kids whose Mummy or Daddy has died, like me. There were lots of different things for us to do there. Mummy went too but she was with the grown-ups. They had their own bit to go to, not with us. At the club they told us about having a 'bag of tricks'. Just for me

(Continued)

(Continued)

to help me feel better if I feel worried. I didn't want to say that I felt scared but some of the others said they sometimes did. I was surprised, that was like me.

If I wake up in the night and don't like the dark corners in my bedroom, I could open my bag of tricks. (It's not a real bag, just pretend, but I put happy thoughts of Daddy in it.) I can remember nice things or funny things about Daddy. (It's OK to think funny things about people who have died, they don't mind.) I remembered when Daddy took me to the park to play football and he kicked the ball very hard and it went into the pond. He said some naughty words and had to take off his shoes and socks and pull his trousers right up and walk into the pond to get my ball, but the water was very cold and he kept making funny faces. It made me laugh. I also made a special box that I can keep special things that belonged to Daddy in. I painted it blue because Daddy liked Chelsea football team and it has lots of footballs and a picture of Daddy on it. Mummy helped me.

Mummy and I sometimes talk about Daddy and the things we used to do. I like to look at Daddy's picture. Sometimes I feel sad, but Mummy said that that is OK.

Dilemmas for the health visitor

There are four dilemmas discussed in this chapter. The first is related to the fact that every child and family is different and their story is exclusive and individual. Consequently each child situation is unique. Following on from this, the child should not be seen in isolation but as part of a family. The whole family is undergoing a transition, so consequently the bereaved child lives in a bereaved family. The third dilemma relates to providing a holistic approach to supporting bereaved families, which necessitates good multi-agency working, though this can be challenging. The final one is related to professional awareness that this difficult subject can evoke personal emotions within professionals working with the family.

Every child and family is different

The uniqueness of each child's story dictates the need to assess and support each situation individually. To support their needs requires a understanding of the impact of this transition (bereavement) on children and their care givers by the professionals working with the family enabling them to signpost or refer the family to appropriate services as individual needs suggest.

There is no right way to grieve; the outpouring of emotional and physical symptoms are common following the death of a loved one. A variety of emotions could be described as normal grief and are an inevitable aspect of the bereavement process. The majority of bereaved adults and children traverse this process without much professional intervention (Childhood Bereavement Network, 2010).

However, some do experience difficulties and their transition can become complicated or stuck. These children have also been identified as being at a significantly higher risk of behaviour and mental health issues in later life (Shear, 2009). The challenge therefore for professionals working with these families is to find innovative and beneficial ways of assisting and supporting in a way that best fits that family (DfES, 2003; Way, 2010).

The child should not be seen in isolation but as part of a family

Children's experiences of their transitions are embedded in their future health and well-being. Their care givers are pivotal to supporting and guiding them through these transitions; children need their love and support to navigate these changes to enable them to flourish and bloom. However, bereaved children live in bereaved families. It is important to recognise that a care giver's capacity to support and guide can be reduced or lost in these circumstances (Vogler et al., 2008; Bonanno, 2009).

In the case of Polly's grandmother, the events had also been traumatic for her as she was grieving the sudden and unexpected loss of a daughter. Additionally, she had to adjust to the sudden and complete change of her own life circumstances, as well as the future life she had planned for herself. She sometimes expressed this distress in statements such as 'I don't think I can do this' and 'I didn't expect to be doing this', and also struggled with her feeling of anger – 'How could she have done this to Polly?' – and then guilt at being angry with her deceased daughter.

A holistic approach to supporting bereaved families

Families do not live in isolation but are a part of a community and society. This community of schools, health and local agencies can provide a holistic approach to supporting children and their families, thereby promoting children's future health and well-being.

However, delivering a holistic approach is not without its problems. A holistic and integrated approach requires collaboration which can be difficult to achieve partly because of the different demands services have on their already limited and valuable time (Rehal, 2008). The sharing of information too can be ethically challenging, as different professionals work to different codes of practice (Hyman, 2008; NMC, 2008). Brocklehurst (2004) promotes collaborative working to develop a greater range of services, which provides children and their families with more choice. The Common Assessment Framework (CAF) is a significant part of the government's Every Child Matters programme and aims to identify, at the earliest opportunity, any unmet need and to co-ordinate service provision to address them (DfES, 2003).

In the cases discussed, the immediate needs of the family were identified and integrated strategies put into place to support the families. This included support from the local Sure-Start and outreach workers, nursery and school staff, bereavement counsellors, the health visitor and even the football coach. This resulted in good multi-agency working that benefited the families and produced a constructive foundation for future collaborative working with them, for the medium and long term.

In these studies the multi-agency teams performed well with the only difficulties encountered being professional time restraints and geographical locality of the meetings. Difficulties relating to confidentiality were overcome by including the parent/guardian within the team, and in all decision making.

Personal emotions within professional working

When supporting bereaved families, professional and support staff need to be mindful that the subject may evoke painful and possibly difficult memories in themselves, which they had thought were resolved or perhaps even forgotten. The process of transition takes place on several levels. This can be within us, with others in the community, as well as with the deceased person (Silverman, 2000).

Several members of the multi-agency team discussed feelings that had been evoked within them and expressed empathetic reactions of their personal reaction as parents or grandparents. It is therefore important to be mindful of these considerations when working with bereaved families.

The health visitor's perspective

Health visitors are uniquely placed to promote and lead this multi-agency integrated team as they are autonomous practitioners, advising and supporting families and children. Leadership in health visiting is not hierarchical but part of their professional responsibility (DoH, 2011). Government initiatives (DfES, 2003; DoH, 2009a), promote a more integrated approach to addressing unmet needs and support children to achieve their full potential.

Working in multi-agency teams can be difficult and demanding as different agencies have different work policies and procedures, which can challenge or even inhibit any collaborative working. The sharing of confidential information can also be ethically challenging, with different agencies working to different codes of practice (Hyman, 2008; NMC, 2008). However, the advantage of good multi-agency working has been confirmed by research to benefit both children and their families, improving well-being and school achievements (Milbourne et al., 2003). To help identify at the earliest opportunity any unmet needs and to help co-ordinate service provision to address these, the Common Assessment Framework (CAF) was a significant assessment tool for these families.

Reflections

Health visitors are in an excellent position to support and instigate innovative, inspired ways of supporting children and their families but they must have the enthusiasm to rise to the challenges of leading an integrated service (Thurtle, 2007). In my opinion, there is definitely a growing need for more collaborative partnerships working to support families, different agencies working and training together in a more comprehensive way to providing a robust, diverse and integrated service that addresses families' individual requirements.

'Integrated working is much more than simply "working together". It is about producing an environment of trust and cooperation where agencies share information and responsibility to become truly client focused' (Rehal, 2008: 43).

My experiences illustrated in the case studies have given me the chance to reflect on not only my own leadership skills but also my collaborative working and provided an opportunity to 'walk' in other services' 'moccasins', which has been unique and empowering (Jasper and Jumaa, 2005). We are in a period of change and re-evaluation, which will affect health, children's services and education. The National Health Service is currently undergoing various changes (DoH 2007, 2009b, 2011) and the need for good leadership to initiate and supervise the necessary changes is essential to deliver a universal and consistent service to all service users.

'However, to learn to be a proficient leader, we must first learn, think and reflect about how we should do things differently. If we don't learn to think and do things differently, we will not change' (Martin, 2003: 1).

Stop Press! Update on the case study

Following this intervention, Matt's mother discussed how she had seen a 'change in him' and said that he seemed livelier now. 'In a good way, he seems more relaxed now.' Polly has needed additional support with moving to a new home and starting school. However due to the collaborative working that was initiated this support was easily accessed and implemented.

CAF was a significant assessment tool for the families in this case study. Also through working in partnership with other agencies, a greater understanding of each other's role was developed and this has consequently continued to benefit the service users.

📖 Further Reading

Silverman, P.R. (2000) *Never Too Young to Know: Death in Children's Lives*. Oxford: Oxford University Press.
This book uses children's own stories to give a practical and theoretical approach to how children cope with death, as well as giving strategies to support children.

Varley, S. (1992) *Badger's Parting Gifts*. London: Collins Picture Lions.
This is an illustrated book for children in which a much-loved badger dies. The story does not conceal the feeling of sadness that comes

with death; however, it also evokes positive attitudes to dealing with such a topic and is an excellent way to introduce the topic to young children.

Ward, B. (1995) *Good Grief: Exploring Feelings, Loss and Death with under Elevens – A Holistic Approach.* London and Bristol, PA: Jessica Kingsley Publishers.

This has remained an essential book for professionals working with children experiencing loss for years. It challenges some of the assumptions that are made about children's feelings in such circumstances and starts from the premise that children need to mourn and know that others respect their need and right to do so. Barbara Ward argues that this will enable them to cope with their own grief or sadness and in turn help them to become more compassionate, understanding people.

Additional resources and educational material can be obtained through bereavement charities such as Childhood Bereavement Charity and Winston's Wish. They provide a wide range of educational information and advice for professionals as well as support for the families and children themselves.

13

Accessing support through outreach

Dulcie Hiscott

Chapter Overview

This chapter explores how a child's transition can be supported by an outreach worker based in a children's centre. The primary purpose of this role is to engage families so that they access services that have the potential to help them improve their lives. However, the role of outreach worker is relatively new. Many professionals working with young children do not know it exists or, at best, do not understand what an outreach worker does. Some professionals perceive the role as a threat to their own professional heritage (Anning et al., 2006). The case study in this chapter offers the reader insight into the work of an outreach worker and the way she works with a child and family referred to the children's centre by the health visitor. The family becomes part of the outreach worker's case load. The outreach worker works directly with the family through home visits and centre-based contacts to support those who have been identified as being in the greatest need of targeted and universal children's centre services. The latter can include postnatal sessions, parenting programmes, advice and support for housing and/or educational needs, benefits and finance. This work involves a voluntary agreement from families that we are able to share information with other agencies such as health or social care in order to provide a multi-agency approach to safeguarding and improving outcomes for children in a holistic framework.

Introduction to the case study

At an initial meeting with a client family it is good practice for the outreach worker to clarify her role and the constraints and possibilities of her work. In this case, the outreach worker makes it clear that her role is to offer support to the parent and emphasises that as someone from the children's centre she has a duty of care to the children with respect to safeguarding. Good practice requires the outreach worker to request and gain written permission from the client that will allow her to discuss the case with other agencies (Oates, 2006).

This transition appeared to be one of moving from universal services to targeted services and safeguarding. The parent had presented with facial injuries that indicated possible domestic violence. There were concerns about what the child had witnessed and whether the mother had the capacity to keep the child safe from harm.

 **Case study**

James (aged four): A lady called an outreach worker came to my school. Mrs Bourne (the teacher) said she was taking me to Mummy, because Mummy was poorly. Is she a social services lady because sometimes Mummy says if I am bad they will take me away? Mrs Bourne told the lady that I had hit my friend, and that she had to tell Mummy, Mummy will be cross, my tummy feels all wobbly, perhaps she won't tell Mummy because she is not cross, she just asked if I am ok. I look up at the lady she has a smiley face and shiny shoes. The lady talks to my mummy. I don't say anything and neither does Mummy. She didn't ask about my day so I won't have to tell her I was sad, and worried because she was hitting out, shouty and cross this morning and I got scared and someone took my toy. I was playing with it when they took it. I wanted that toy. He made me cross so I hit him. That's what you do when you get cross. You hit people. Then they stop. I wanted him to stop and he stopped then he cried. But I don't care because he took my toy. Mummy keeps saying to the lady – I've had enough and they need to do something. When Mummy says a bad word the lady's face goes all funny and Mummy says sorry but she's stressed. Mummy gets cross when she is stressed. Mummy will be cross if the lady tells her about the boy who took my toy.

(Continued)

(Continued)

I look at Mummy. She is holding her hurting face. I hope the doctor will make it better, and then Mummy won't be sad and cross. The smiley lady is talking to my Mummy. Lots of grown-ups talk to Mummy and they all have their pictures on a necklace. I am playing in the toy house at the hospital and I keep looking at that smiley lady to see if she tells my mum about the boy who took my toy. She is talking to Mummy. I can hear her. She is telling Mummy. She is telling her. She said I hit another child. She didn't tell Mummy he took my toy. She said some big words. My tummy is going all jelly. Mummy will be cross. She will be all shouty again. What if she gets angry? Why did I hit the boy? Mrs Bourne didn't tell her he took the toy.

I don't want Mummy to get mad again. I love Mummy. I am scared. I'm going over. I am walking little steps. If I keep my head down then they won't see me. The smiley lady isn't smiley. Is she cross too? She tells Mummy to talk to Mrs Bourne. I stand in front of Mummy. I keep my head down. I am scared. If I tell Mummy I love her she might not get mad. So I look up with my eyes at Mummy's eyes. Mummy looks away so I put my hands on Mummy's face and stroke her face all soft all the way to the bottom and I look right in her beautiful eyes. I say I love you Mummy but she does not see me or hear me. Please hear me, Mummy. If I love you, you can be happy and not cross. I stroke my mummy's face so gentle because she is poorly. I look at Mummy and tell her I love her again. Mummy pulls my hands down and pushes them away. She says 'Yeah I love you', but I can't see her beautiful eyes because they are not looking...

Outreach worker: The language used by James – 'I love you Mummy' – and the response from his mother – 'Yeah, I love you' – seemed to say so much. The mother's tone of voice, body language and use of the word 'Yeah' undermined the 'I love you' element of what she said. The short interaction between the mother and child suggests a lack of warmth and attunement from the mother and intense anxiety and insecurity on the part of James. He seems to be desperately attempting to appease his mother and is perhaps concerned about how to please her and also how to avoid her disapproval. James's behaviour is his way of communicating his feelings and needs. It might suggest the presence of emotional abuse which may be 'doing significant harm' to the child.

Having witnessed this episode I am concerned about this child. I need to complete a home visit in order find out more and enable the whole family to access some appropriate support services. I don't know how the mother may react though and I do not want to put myself at risk of harm if there is violence and aggression in the family. Also I feel that my lack of knowledge about the case could potentially impact upon my effectiveness in the home visit as well as my personal safety. I think I will approach the child's health visitor for a case history.

Later

In light of this, I contacted the health visitor and requested an historical overview of this particular client family. I hoped that she would share details that highlight deeper issues and give a context for this family. I felt that this was an appropriate request in terms of both my professional effectiveness and my personal safety. This would ultimately impact on the outcomes for this family. However, she responded: 'What are you hoping for? You have to be realistic about what this client can achieve!' I felt that this response indicated that she was unsure of my professional status, had a limited view of the expectations for this family and little sense of the potential of what could be achieved through working with this family. I further felt this response could be seen as a pre-judged subjective assumption of both the families parenting capacity and my professional competencies.

My immediate thought was, 'How can I support this child and family effectively if information is not shared with me?' I could now clearly see my important new leadership role for this family, potentially providing a fresh approach to family support leadership. For the family, then, this outreach role could appear to be 'a communicator' working with them to support effective multi-agency working and information sharing.

The next morning

Outreach worker: Due to the response from the health visitor and the level of my concern, the children's centre manager has arranged for me to attend the health visitors' team meeting. I can argue that if they expect me to work with this difficult client, they have a duty of care towards me. So, in order to support this family, I need other professionals to share information with me. I'll rehearse what I am going to say in the car before arriving because I need to choose my words carefully. It will be important to get it right because whatever I say might influence the outcome of the meeting and therefore the children involved. I need to be assertive to maintain any professional credibility that I have!

(Continued)

(Continued)

After the meeting

Outreach worker (speaking to the children's centre manager after the meeting): Phew! I was glad I rehearsed what I was going to say. When I saw a chance I began a discussion with the health team around the sharing of this information. At one point I stated that the health visitors had an ethical responsibility to share information with other professionals in order to safeguard the well-being of everyone involved. When I said this, the health visitor manager asked everyone to be quiet and requested that I repeat what I had just said. I think this was a turning point.

From this moment, the necessary information was willingly shared. I felt they accepted me as a fellow professional. By drawing on a concern shared by everyone working with children and expressing myself in language common to us all, I had found a way to work collaboratively with the health visitors in order to support the family. The latter informed me that the undefined outreach role would not be determined solely by me, but by the leadership challenges that lay before me (Usher et al., 1997). By this I mean that my ability to communicate with professionals in a preferred language would determine the level of professional credibility that they would afford me and my role in a multi-agency team.

A week later

Outreach worker: Now that I have gathered more information via the health visitors I am concerned that James is at risk of far more harmful issues. Emotional abuse is commonly linked to other forms of abuse. In this instance, the information received from the health visitors suggests there might also be neglect. I am aware of advice from the National Society for the Prevention of Cruelty to Children (2009) that emotional abuse is notoriously difficult to prove and its effects are often carried through to adulthood. The past will map out the future for James (Harper et al., 2003) but how can I, as an outreach worker, intervene to prevent it?

Gathering all of the information together including the information relating to historical domestic violence, the interprofessional team of which I am part has suggested that this family makes the transition from universal services like those generally available from the children's centre to targeted services and child protection safeguarding. It was agreed that a CAF (Common Assessment Frame) would be offered to the client family and the health visitor and I would do a joint visit to the client family's home. It became apparent to the health visitor and I during this visit that the parent was experiencing a high level of anxiety. This presented itself in the form of volatile and aggressive outbursts during the visit. The CAF process was offered to the parent as a means by which she could access support and funding for services or items that would improve outcomes for her children. The parent declined this offer; however, she did agree to access the children's centre in times of distress.

The health visitor and I worked together contacting charities to access funding for basic equipment for the family, i.e. a washing machine and carpets. In my outreach role I contacted a local after school provider who agreed a reduced rate so that James could access a safe and secure play environment. The funding for this session was accessed by me through a local charity. The parent was invited to attend additional adult-led play sessions at the centre with her younger child.

These interventions were put into place in order to address the needs of the child, which were viewed by the health visitor and me to be issues of a safeguarding nature. Due to our feelings about what could be happening for the child, we made referrals to children's services. Finally, following these interventions and a children's services investigation, the children were placed on the child protection register.

Dilemmas for the outreach worker

Disadvantage passes down the generations

Harper et al. (2003) suggest that it is not just being disadvantaged by poverty that tends to transfer from one generation to another. We should include 'Human capital (such as education, coping strategies, physical health or disease): attitudes, cultural and other knowledge' (Harper et al., 2003: 536). Interrupting this transmission of disadvantage from the mother to the child offered a chance to intervene in the lives of everyone in the family and improve their life chances. One intervention that can be made is to empower children by supporting their transitions.

There are many ways to 'listen'

Although everyone working with children is required to consult individual children in order to gain their views about their lives, this often proves to be difficult. Robinson suggests, 'It is up to us to carefully observe the child, notice the context, behaviour and/or appearance which may give clues as to how the child might be feeling' (2008: 172).

If we are to do that effectively we need to be trained in observation techniques, have experience of children and an understanding of child development alongside having access to a professional community who can provide professional supervision and a community of practice in which to discuss cases confidentially.

The way we hear and share the voice of the child needs care; for example:

> 'I stroke my Mummy's face so gentle because she is poorly. I look at Mummy and tell her I love her again. Mummy pulls my hands down and pushes them away. She says 'Yeah I love you', but I can't see her beautiful eyes because they are not looking.'

This gives a greater sense of how the child feels rather than the language used in a report, such as this:

> The child seems to be desperately attempting to appease her mother and is perhaps concerned about how to please her and also how to avoid her disapproval.

The way we document incidents and share information can prevent the voice of the child being heard. If we lose the child's voice through the way we create documentation, we may lose the ability to find creative solutions to support the child's life chances and well-being.

Professional hierarchies should not get in the way

There needs to be transparency and information sharing between professionals working with a client family. This also has to include the family itself. The voice of all who have contact with the client family, be it the teaching assistant or the social worker, must be valued in a non-hierarchical manner if the child's best interests are to be served. It is important to be inclusive of the family too. *The Working Together to Safeguard Guidance* states:

> The local authority has a responsibility to make sure children and adults have all the information they require to help them understand the processes that are followed where there are concerns about a child's welfare. Information should be clear and accessible and available in the family's preferred language. (Department of Children, Schools and Families, 2010: 286)

In the case study, the outreach worker managed to pull other professionals together by arguing for mutual accountability (Wenger, 1998). One of the difficulties of supporting transitions is the tendency of professionals to remain in their 'silos'. Duplication and a lack of co-ordination may mean that the various professionals concerned with a case undermine the work of others by sending mixed messages to the child and family. It is worth remembering that families tend to be unaware of professional differences, so sharing experiences and information helps to avoid misunderstandings and opportunities for clients to be manipulative.

Evidence-based judgements from a multi-agency team

It is difficult to maintain one's confidence in having the right to make potentially life-changing judgements about other human beings. However, the judges of 'normality' are present everywhere. Our society is made up of teacher-judges, doctor-judges, educator-judges and social worker-judges, to name but a few professional roles, and they control the normative rules of conduct (Foucault, 1979). What are the criteria for being 'normal' and through whose eyes should we be looking? A multi-professional team can create a stronger and more focused, evidence-based and child-centred view of what is 'normal' than a single professional who may doubt whether their view is partial or cultural.

The outreach worker's perspectives

An essential element of my role in this case study was to take a strength-based approach to meeting the needs of the children within the client family. In order to achieve this, it was vital to assess what was happening currently for this family appropriately. This meant that the health visitor and I, when visiting the family at home, had to combine our knowledge of historical and current factors involved in this family's needs and investigate the resources available to meet these needs within the local area and at the children's centre.

As I worked with the family to develop an action plan that they agreed could potentially meet their needs, I was very aware that I should help the family to do, rather than to be done to. In this consultative process my role became leader, facilitator – middle person, partner, friend, enemy, multi-agency practitioner, family advocate and translator as dictated by the needs of the family.

Reflections

In order to support the child and family as they experience a transition, a combination of leadership skills is needed. One skill is to listen, really listen, to other professionals who are also working with the client family (Covey, 2004). Professional trust and collaboration, effective communication and sharing are key approaches needed to facilitate interprofessional working. In particular safeguarding responsibilities require professionals to communicate effectively and join together all the pieces of information. They need to recognise that they are not capable of resolving issues alone from within their professional teams and that there are great benefits from retaining multiple truths and insights in a multi-agency team.

Stop Press! Update on the case study

There is evidence to suggest that things have improved for the children within this client family. The family have accessed quality childcare provision in the local area with the assistance of charity funding, sourced by myself. Additionally, the parent continues to access the centre for support and clarity with regard to what is happening for her and her family within the multi-agency framework of her support. Furthermore, positive relationships have been forged with the health team, children's services, local childcare providers and the education sector. These newly forged relationships have supported the family in accessing a multi-agency approach to understanding and meeting their needs. Finally, the family remain on the child-protection register. However, the mother is now working positively and in partnership with the professionals who endeavour to reflect back to her how they see the world from her children's perspectives.

📖 Further Reading

Beckett, C. (2007) *Child Protection: An Introduction*, 2nd edn. London: Sage.
Beckett offers readers a sound guide to child-protection issues and dilemmas. This writer explores case studies, which illuminate the impact of negative and damaging intergenerational transitions for children.

Claxton, G. (1998) *Hare Brain, Tortoise Mind*. London: Fourth Estate Limited.
This book offers an understanding of how we can learn by being absorbed in a particular situation. It guides us towards slow thinking as a means of finding clarity when faced with complexity.

Fullan, M. (2001) *Leading in a Culture of Change*. San Francisco: Jossey-Bass.
Fullan examines the complex nature of leading through a time of change and uncertainty. In doing so, he explores emotional intelligence, slow knowing and moral purpose, which can offer guidance to outreach workers and professionals working with children and families.

14

Becoming an outreach worker

Jennifer Lee McStravick

Chapter Overview

Transitions combine turning points, milestones or life events with subtle, complex processes of 'becoming somebody' personally, educationally and occupationally. Such processes are sometimes a response to particular events, and sometimes events arise out of shifts and developments in identity and agency (Ecclestone, 2007: 3). This chapter uses an example of an outreach worker in a children's centre to explore the concept of transition experienced by someone working in one of the new roles that have emerged in work with children. The role and purpose of a children's centre outreach worker are not generally understood and vary from one centre to another, not just in relation to the community the centre serves, but to the individual in post, staff team, lead agencies and professional background. This chapter is written from the perspective of someone who is experiencing a transition from her previous work role to the role of an outreach worker. The case study identifies some good practice that supports staff who are experiencing similar transitions themselves while at the same time working with children and families who are also experiencing transitions.

Introduction to the case study

One of the key roles in a children's centre is an outreach worker. However, as Dulcie Hiscott writes in Chapter 13, the role is not understood or established. This case study looks at the experiences of an outreach worker named Poonam who is trying to do her best for her client families while in an uncertain, ambiguous job role.

 ## Leaving outreach work

Poonam: I worked in another area of the country previously. We had a co-ordinator at the children's centre rather than a manager. She co-ordinated three children's centres and frankly you weren't supported and things happened that should not have happened. We didn't have a manager there all the time. There was one other full-time support worker there. She had been in post for a few months. I actually hated it. You didn't know whether you were coming or going. There was no-one actually to direct or guide you yet there were some very critical moments – and sometimes things did not go smoothly. I felt I muddled through each day. I had a job description but what I did depended on the co-ordinator. The actual job description said that you were doing outreach but you did not actually do that job. So the role was very different to the job description. I was unclear about my role. This seemed a common story. Those who had been in the role a bit longer found the role was not what they took on. When other professional became involved I did not know what was happening and if I should be doing something more to assist the family. I worked with a family – not doing home visits – but I worked with the family for a year before I found out by accident that they were on the Child Protection Register. I just didn't feel we were kept in the loop. I felt cross and very upset. I spoke about it to the co-ordinator but I felt that she did not understand how important it was. I felt I was being criticised for not doing what she wanted me to do but then she did not keep me in the loop about important matters.

I feel strongly that you should know what is going on with a family. That's what makes me think it is down to the individual children's centre co-ordinators. There should be clear guidance about what we should know and do and who should tell us. There is a big gap in who is monitoring what managers and co-ordinators are doing with staff. Obviously we have our SEFs (Self-Evaluation Forms) at each centre but that does not look at staff turnaround and supervision, etc.

My coping mechanism was to leave and look for a role as a deputy manager in the day-care in another children's centre. At the time I said I would never do outreach again. When I had my exit interview the co-ordinator was off sick so I had the interview with her line manager. I told her why

(Continued)

(Continued)

I was leaving after quite a short time. She didn't say much really. She just said it should not be like that. Before I took the next job, when my next manager rang me up and said that I had got the job, I had a long chat with him before I accepted the post. For example, I said to him that I felt home visits were essential. I needed to be clear where I stood. I took the trouble to check we agreed on most things before I actually accepted the job.

Back to outreach work

Poonam: When I left that job as an outreach worker I took a post working as a deputy manager at the day-care in this children's centre. One day the children's centre manager rang me up and said she was looking for an outreach worker and would I consider applying. When I had my interview for this new outreach role my understanding was that I would start by learning how to do baby massage and I would be supporting the drop-in groups. I was relieved that I knew what was required and I was very excited to come back to outreach work. I felt confident. I was already the designated person for child protection at the day-care and that role transferred with me. Everything felt very smooth and natural.

Changes to the role of outreach worker

Poonam: Obviously things changed quite a lot when we were required to try to draw in 'hard to reach' families and as the outreach worker I was going out promoting the children's centre across the local community and doing home visits. It was a new approach in this centre and everyone was excited about it and I was as well. Everyone in the children's centre was interested in how this approach to the role was going to work because nobody actually really knew. My manager said to me, 'Right, this is a new way of working and we need someone to explore it. Can you do it?' That made it quite exciting. I was given a free rein to do whatever I wanted in the role. Initially I ran 'stay and play' sessions, went out promoting the centre and made myself known at toddler groups. I started working with some childminders and supporting them in implementing the Early Years Foundation Stage (EYFS). That's probably beyond what I was expected to do but it is something I am able to do successfully because of my background. It was rewarding for me because I was able to bring my existing skills to the new version of the role. The freedom and the flexibility of being an outreach worker is actually what is lovely about it and to be honest 80 per cent of the time you spend your time being nice to people. How many people get to do that at work! You focus on things that help people and support them. Access to my help is voluntary so people want my help and support when I start work with them. I'm not pressurising people to do things or anything like that. I am really aware it is a privilege to be invited into people's homes.

There is a great culture here. In team meetings I have a chance to have a say and it is just a professional conversation really. We work together. I feel like my professional opinion is being respected. If I say I think a family needs more support the team listen to me.

A manager needs to have time for their staff, understand the area of work properly, not least so they can offer supervision regarding the case work, and be approachable. At team meetings we can share workloads and gripes – practical and emotional stuff – but in case we might want to moan about the manager or each other, he has just recruited an outside organisation to offer us work-based counselling for two hours per month. We can increase it to four hours or decrease it to one hour (it is our choice) but we have to have one hour per month. It helps us offload if we have difficult cases not necessarily about the case but just the emotional stuff. My manager sees it as a way of caring for the carers.

I feel we are making a difference; for example, we have managed to get parents to attend sessions here at the children's centre and we have got parents to go on parenting courses. It helps that I have had the chance to go on a lot of training, for instance the integrated practice one workshop and the information sharing course, safeguarding – you can go on virtually anything if you think it will develop you in your role. One of the best things is the chance to meet up with other outreach workers – to network.

This job is very different to my previous one because you can actually see outcomes from your work because you are working as a big team. You can see things changing whereas before you did not see anything changing. You engaged with a family and then you lost touch with the case. Because we work as team I can keep in touch with how a child and family are doing. I do have a bit of a passion for my job. It is quite rewarding. Before I did not feel respected and valued. This isn't easy work, you know. I had a friend who worked in the same area that she lived in and she was actually assaulted in the supermarket by a dad. So far the parents here seem to see me as part of the community so there have not been any problems, thank goodness.

Outreach work varies though. Some outreach workers run stay/play sessions while others are doing home visits and working with families in serious difficulties. Some are facilitating parenting sessions and have an awareness of

(Continued)

(Continued)

adult learning needs while others just set up a meeting between a support group and let it happen. Everyone is lumped together. That is an issue in our relationships with other agencies because it means there is confusion about what they can ask an outreach worker to do. The role is so blurred it creates problems.

In my new job at the moment I am doing lots of outreach and going into people's homes. However, I know that there are other children's centres where they are not responding to any of the outreach work. That is quite important because I have to go into the home and get people in to come into the children's centre to engage with activities. I have to work with them in the home and build up their confidence first. You can't just expect so called 'hard to reach families' to turn up – if they did they would be called 'easy to reach'! They are not going to come in without support. Tomorrow I am taking one of the mums to a session because she says she is only comfortable to come in because she trusts me.

I don't think people value the outreach service and understand what it is we do. Some other professionals have wanted me to be a 'gofer' just doing their CAF (Common Assessment Framework) administration. They don't ask me to do any outreach work because they are unsure about outreach. The outreach role is so broad and complex that you could be dealing with many different types of situation. You have to be able to manage and lead those situations appropriately and that means that you have to adapt your practices to suit. I have gone from a situation where I am having a conversation with a speech and language therapist, then supporting the childminders and the next thing I have got a parent 'effing and blinding' at me! You have got to be able to switch from one thing to another suddenly because that is the nature of the job. Oh, then after all of that I have got to talk with a health visitor and tell them about the parent in an appropriate way and it all has to be documented, transferring that information correctly and appropriately.

Outreach workers know that everybody you meet is going to be different and their needs are going to be different. It doesn't work to have a generic tick list in your head. You need to pull in other people to support the family and be open to other people's ideas so you can move this family forward. No-one has all the answers.

Dilemmas for the managers of outreach workers

Defining the role of outreach worker

The role of the 'outreach worker' is too broad and requires some clarity and better definition if post holders are to be effective. As Jarvis and Trodd argue, in order to contribute, an individual in a multi-agency team 'must have a clear understanding of his or her knowledge, skills, beliefs and values' (2008: 214)

In her first outreach job, Poonam was not given a job description that reflected the role she was asked to undertake. The effect of this was made worse by lack of understanding about her role from her line manager, peers and partners in other agencies. There are different types of outreach role with very different levels of accountability, expertise and impact. The role is varied so pay needs to reflect the level of responsibility and accountability.

A concern is that a majority of outreach workers do not have social work qualifications, relevant supervision or training or experience. They cope with the demands of the job by using communication skills and good will.

Being part of a team

Flexibility in a role enables staff to feel valued and have enjoyment in their role and develops their resilience to cope with the unknown. However, the emotional demands of undertaking a new, uncertain role should not be overlooked and relevant supervision and peer support are required. Ideally, the post holder should work in a team or network of outreach workers so they can share their experiences and skills, bounce ideas off each other and work together to support the complex needs of client families.

Support and training

Children's centre managers should be accountable to the lead agency and the local authority for providing the supervision, induction and support needed by outreach workers. They will need to receive training themselves in order to do this and there will be budget implications for the children's centre. A named qualification for the role would reflect the importance of the role, value the experiences of outreach workers and enable them to combine their knowledge of practical work with theory and systems. Such a qualification would help to ensure that outreach workers are able to work safely. As Finch et al. write, 'If, for example, some children's centre outreach workers are expected to undertake work with families where there are safeguarding concerns, this will have implications for their training, support and supervision' (2009: 7).

The outreach worker perspectives

If you asked me for three wishes as an outreach worker, they would be as follows.

First, I would like an actual purpose-built centre. At the moment it is a bit of a nightmare as we rent an office on one side of the road and we rent a disused church on the other side of the road but we cannot have them all the time as there are other things going on, naturally. It is very difficult actually getting people to places. Our office is tiny – probably the size of a bathroom. There is only room for two desks, a photo-copier and a cupboard. I wanted to get sand and water trays for the children's play sessions but we can't when you are just renting space.

Second, I think a qualification for outreach workers would be good. It might mean that we would get more respect from other professionals and recognition from them. That isn't just because I think we deserve more respect, it is because if other professionals recognise what we do, there is more chance that they will share essential information with us and include us in the 'Team Around the Family' work. It will help us to help the children and families more effectively. I think the problem with the outreach role is that it is vague and it seems to depend on who walks in the door! You cannot cover everything with one lot of training. We need access to the high-level child-protection training but it might scare people from the role. They might wonder – do I get paid enough to do a role in which children's lives and well-being are in my hands? I don't want to be melodramatic but I do make life-changing decisions about children in my role. Social ser-vices are not able to engage as much as they used to because they are under so much pressure and I find myself picking up some of their responsibilities. If you explained that to someone who applied for the job thinking they were going to be running stay and play ses-sions, would they take the job? I doubt it.

Third, I'd like more clarity about what outreach workers are supposed to do, who we're accountable to, who our managers are accountable to, and whether we are supposed to receive an induction and supervi-sion. I'd like to work as part of a team of outreach workers instead of being isolated.

A few years ago my manager was a participant of the National Professional Qualification for Integrated Centre Leadership (known as NPQICL), a nationally recognised qualification for all centre managers.

The outcome of that study for her was clarity regarding differences between a manager and a leader, and acceptance of her own leadership qualities and reflective practices. This reflective process is now embedded into her work and she devotes as much time to reflecting back on her work as she does to forward planning. She finds reflective practice enlightening, allowing her to accept mistakes as part of her learning and to acknowledge the importance of the process as well as the desired outcomes or a project or piece of work. This is a vital skill for outreach workers in Sure-Start.

Stop Press! Update on the case study

Since the comprehensive budget review by the coalition government, many local authorities, support agencies, charity and voluntary sector groups have received budget cuts, reducing their capacity to engage and work in partnership. In addition many organisations have streamlined their focus and increased thresholds for referrals for their support. In practice this has had an impact on the nature of the cases/families that the outreach roles are encountering. Families who were previously supported by a named social worker through statutory interventions (such as child protection or supervision orders) are now frequently not meeting the higher threshold for social care intervention. Families who could have been helped to access local charity or voluntary groups are now facing closing groups or that they no longer meet the eligibility criteria. This means the outreach sector are working with family cases and situations that previously required work from a qualified social worker or from other agencies. This has led to rapid up-skilling and upheaval for those in an outreach post, and a reduction in the universal 'delivery' aspects of their role. As yet it is too soon to judge if this is sustainable, effective or acceptable.

📖 Further Reading

Anning, A., Cottrell, D., Frost, N., Green, J. and Robinson, M. (2010) *Developing Multiprofessional Teamwork for Integrated Children's Services: Research, Policy and Practice*. Maidenhead: Open University Press.

This is a useful study into the initial development of inter-agency and interprofessional working. It explores how multi-professional workers develop their professional identity through their integrated practice and involvement in multi-professional teams.

Siraj-Blatchford, I., Clarke, K. and Needham, M. (2007) *The Team around the Child: Multi-agency Working in the Early Years*. Stoke-on-Trent: Trentham Books.

Taking a comprehensive look at the barriers and issues when working with integrated services, partnership and children's services, this is a relevant text for new senior outreach staff and centre managers.

Trodd, L. and Chivers, L. (2011) *Interprofessional Working in Practice: Learning and Working Together for Children and Families*. Maidenhead: Open University Press.

Part 3: 'Working' in this book offers an interesting take on transition and safeguarding with references to the Munro Review and green papers since 2010.

Conclusion

Lyn Trodd

The role of the transition worker

Some of the transitions in the case studies in this book are a normal part of every child's life and probably experienced by all families. Several of them are unexpected transitions and are less common but nevertheless occur every day, somewhere to someone. Children, families and practitioners who experience challenging transitions are often resilient and come through them stronger than ever, having learned a great deal about themselves and how to be in the world in the process. When that is not the case professionals, like the authors in this book, are part of the team of transition workers who may be able to intervene to provide an interprofessional safety net to support a transitioning child and family. Some of the case studies illustrate occasions when this safety net is provided *reactively* when things are already going wrong but others show that much can be done *proactively* so the safety net is not needed.

The voice of the child

In Chapter 12, Pamela Curran describes how the voice of the child can be overlooked and difficult to access in the emotional maelstrom that can occur when there are 'big' events, such as a death in the family. Attention to the 'voice of the child' should be seen as fundamental to respecting the rights of the child rather than just arising out of the child's needs. As such it is not an outcome of benevolent charity on behalf of transition workers but a legal and professional requirement. However, it is perhaps easier to respect a single child's agency and right to participate in his or her own life than those of larger groups of children. A current fallacy that prevails is that children, or parents for that matter, have one voice and that 'the voice of the child' is one universal view. All this fallacy does is to leave room for pre-conceptions by adults about what children want or need. In Chapter 8, Helena Marks argues that transition workers have to be thoughtful and creative in using every means possible to 'hear' the child. In Helena's case study this means accepting that those who live alongside and work with a child with special educational needs and disability (SEND) every day may have better access to the child's views than professionals.

Working across interprofessional boundaries

Rushmer and Pallis discuss integrated working and the danger of 'blurring boundaries' between professionals and conclude that 'simply bringing together and calling a collection of differing professionals a "team", does not guarantee shared tasks and knowledge, integrated interprofessional working, or the seamless delivery of services ... The secret is to maintain clear boundaries but overlap them' (Rushmer and Pallis, 2002: 64). The highest level of interprofessional working is achieved when interprofessionalism is an ontological position (Trodd and Chivers, 2011) that takes an inclusive view of 'other' professionals. Identification with particular professional heritages and adherence to different ways of working can be perceived barriers to integrated working. It is very unhelpful for families to be caught up in the middle of this. After all, what they want is the best outcome for their child and themselves and the additional stress of strained professional relationships can make an already stressful situation worse. Spanning boundaries between agencies and operating effective cross-agency referral processes means resources, information and services can be marshalled when and where they are needed to support the child and family. The transformation this approach can achieve is shown in Chapter 1 when Lydia Ottavio uses her case study to demonstrate the difference made by true interprofessional teamwork.

A particularly important skill for the transition worker is timeliness. Information needs to be shared *before* a child and family transfers into another context or agency. However, as Emma Perry argues in

Chapter 2, information received from another agency will only support the transition if it is received with respect and is put to use. Attention to the needs of the child is lost when a nursery teacher puts aside the information carefully assembled and sent from a pre-school relating to children moving up to nursery saying, 'I know that they have spent hours on this but I don't have the time to read it, and I have to get my own assessments done really quickly after the children start. Anyway the children need a fresh start.' In the meantime, the pre-school leader is wondering whether the effort in creating the transfer information is worth it and thinking, 'We spend ages getting everything ready to send off for the children who are moving up to nurseries. But I know they don't look at it. They just think it's not worth looking at. They ignore it.'

Pre-existing good relationships with other agencies can help the transition worker to find creative solutions to some transition difficulties. 'People work for people – not for visions or strategies or targets – and give of their best when they feel connected' (Binney et al., 2005: 38). It can make a great difference to transitionees if transition workers know about local resources, such as groups, services, information and opportunities. Other important ways practitioners can support transitionees, should further support be necessary, are by understanding appropriate referral routes within their own organisations and making effective links with other practitioners. As Dulcie Hiscott shows in Chapter 13, transition workers have to be aware of the limits of their own roles and be ready to call upon or work with other professionals when a more extensive safety net is needed. Not to do so is to devalue the skills and experience other professionals may have. For instance, teachers are trained to work with children in the main. It requires a different skill set to work with adults and it can feel quite intimidating if it feels a parent is questioning your professionalism and is upset and angry.

Messiness and unpredictability require flexibility

In Chapter 3 Helen Longstaff warns of the dangers of being complacent about transition work. There are no magic formulae or universal processes to be followed. There is value is addressing general structural discontinuities but the crucial tension to be addressed is how far the 'receiving' organisation or service can match what they provide to the current needs of children and their families. In Chapter 5, Julia Bateson's case study uses the grounds of equality of opportunities to make the case for meeting the needs of children and families who are in differing circumstances. Later, in Chapter 11, Mariana Graham demonstrates creative flexibility. She explains how, typically, a critical incident approach is used in serious case reviews in order to identify systemic and individual failing but in her chapter Mariana applies a strengths-based approach based on appreciative inquiry to her child protection work in order to be as constructive as possible in her approach to a complex and difficult case.

Transition workers have to deploy knowledge-in-action accumulated from their professional and life experiences and reflection-in-action defined by Schön (1987) as the ability of professionals to think about what they are doing while they are doing it in order to respond to the complexity and individuality of the transitions they support. This professional artistry and ability to act with autonomy can be seen in the reflections on the discussion of the dilemmas faced by transition workers in each chapter. They also show how transition work can be 'messy' and unpredictable and how the transition worker needs to bear in mind Judi Marshall's advice to interprofessional leaders:

- Let the tentative be tentative.

- Sit with what emerges and don't hold on too tightly. (1994: 174)

One feature of knowledge-in-action that transition workers may draw on is their own experience of messy and unpredictable professional transitions. In Chapter 14 Jennifer Lee McStravick's case study depicts the challenges faced by an outreach worker whose new role is unclear so she has to be resilient and determine her own way of working while she engages with children and families in transition.

Quality of relationships

The quality of relationships is tested during transitions. Where they are open and honest and respectful of the development of the child and the culture of the family the support offered is more likely to be well received and effective. Practitioners may need to draw heavily from the 'emotional piggy bank' held by the transitioning child or family members and hopefully filled beforehand by small accommodations and pleasant exchanges characterised by mutual trust and respect. It is good practice to consult with children and parents about the documentation that is created to support transition. As Helena

Marks suggests in Chapter 8, good proactive communication and information sharing, encouraging optimism and positivity and talking to colleagues require a change of mind-set, open-heartedness and an effort to understand the experiences of others. Little things can make a big difference for transitionees and are practically cost free. Parents attending a case meeting are likely to enter the room in different frames of mind if they have sat for several minutes outside listening to the buzz of conversation from the professionals they are about to meet.

Promoting the agency, self-efficacy and autonomy of the transitionee

In Chapter 7 Alison McLauchlin's moving portrayal of how Steven's mum, Kate, became more and more disempowered through the chain of transitions she experienced following adopting him is an example of potential damage inflicted by poorly supported transitions. When familiarity and continuity are sustained wherever possible, significant others are included in planning a transition and the child and family are encouraged to develop emotional literacy, resilience in transitions can be built. If practitioners are able to decentre and empathise with the child and family, it is possible for them to glimpse experiences of transitions from the transitionees' viewpoints and, as a result, work more sensitively and responsively to provide support. It is important to listen to any worries and to find ways to hear the views of transitionees even when that is not easy.

Some concerns and anxieties can be alleviated by providing the right information in a timely and positive way. Children and families can be greatly reassured if the transition is explained to them in terms they can appreciate. In Chapter 4 Amanda Ricciardi's case study tells how Oliver had no understanding of why he has been left. In Chapter 9 Anne Ross tells of the impact of lack of information, i.e. a diagnosis, on the levels of stress and anxiety experienced by Mr and Mrs Jones as parents of a child with special education needs. Knowing the 'rules' of the new situation or context can ease the process of change considerably. Another approach is to create a 'rehearsal' of some of the threatening circumstances of the transition. In Chapter 6 David Allen explains how he has written a story called 'The Junior Fairy' which he reads to Year 2 children just before they move into the juniors so that the children have a chance to self-conceptualise in the role of a Year 3 pupil. Similarly a nursery school may put school-uniform items in the role-play area so that children can explore the meaning of going to big school in their play or a case worker may talk parents through the procedures involved in a CAF (Common Assessment Framework) meeting.

A transition worker needs to recognise and take account of any signs of changes in the attitudes and behaviour of children and families and in particular to be aware of the cumulative effect of multiple transitions that might be occurring and the effect of a transition when it is added to pre-existing stresses. This aspect of the experience of transition is illustrated in the case studies, particularly in Chapter 10, written by Sally Patterson. One of the challenging aspects of experiencing a transition can be that life seems out of control. Everything may appear to be 'done to' or 'done for' the transitionee. It is worth the practitioner and parent trying to encourage transition-ees to retain their agency and autonomy during the period of change. When children and families have a chance to talk about their concerns there is a chance for practitioners to legitimise them and some-times to reframe them. They should point out the exciting and positive aspects of the changes that are happening. If the transition-ees are consulted, keep making the choices that matter to them about their priorities and have a chance to narrate their versions of the 'stories' of their transition, they are likely to retain some control over their lives and avoid a sense of disempowerment. One of the long-lasting and most destructive effects of a 'bad' transition can be a loss of agency and self-efficacy while a 'good' one can lead to learning, autonomy, resilience and self-belief.

References

ACAS (Advisory, Conciliation and Arbitration Service) (2010) Parental Leave. London: ACAS. www.acas.org.uk/index.aspx?articleid=1637 (accessed 9 May 2010)

Adams, K. and Christenson, S. (2002) Difference in parent–teacher trust levels. Implications for creating collaborative family–school relationships, *Journal of Applied School Psychology Special Services in the Schools*, 14(1/2), 1–22.

Amato, P.R. and Keith, B. (1991) Parental divorce and adult wellbeing: a meta-analysis, *Journal of Marriage and the Family*, 53, 43–58.

Ancona, D., Malone, T., Orlikowski, W. and Senge, P. (2007) In praise of the incompetent leader, *Harvard Business Review*, February, 85(2), 92–100.

Anning, A., Cottrell, D. Frost, N., Green, J. and Robinson, M. (2006) *Developing Multi-Professional Teamwork for Integrated Children's Services*. Maidenhead: Open University Press.

Bandura, A. (1986) *Social Foundation of Thought and Action: A Social Cognitive Theory*. Englewood Cliffs, NJ: Prentice-Hall

Bandura, A. (1994) Self-efficacy, in V.S. Ramachaudran (ed.), *Encyclopedia of Human Behavior*, vol. 4, pp. 71–81, New York: Academic Press. Reprinted in H. Friedman (ed.) (1998) *Encyclopedia of Mental Health*. San Diego: Academic Press.

Bandura, A. (2001) Social cognitive theory: an agentic perspective, *Annual Review of Psychology*, 52, 1–26.

Baras, R. (2010) Parenting expert says happy parents raise happy kids. www.prlog.org/10528860-parenting-expert-says-happy-parents-raise-happy-kids.html (accessed 14 March 2010).

Batty, D. (2011) 'Just 60 babies adopted last year in England'. *The Guardian*, 29 September. www.guardian.co.uk/2011/sep/29/60-babies-adopted-england-last-year (accessed March 2012).

Beckett, C. and Taylor, H. (2010) *Human Growth and Development*, 2nd edn. London: Sage.

Berlin, L., Yair, Z., Amaya-Jackson, L. and Greenberg, M. (eds) (2005) *Enhancing Early Attachments: Theory, Research, Intervention, and Policy*. New York: Guilford Press.

Beveridge, S. (1997) Implementing partnership with parents in schools, in S. Wolfendale (ed.), *Working with Parents of SEN Children after the Code of Practice*. London: Fulton.

Binney, G., Wilke, G. and Williams, C. (2005) *Living Leadership: A Practical Guide for Ordinary Heroes.* Cambridge: Pearson.

Bird, J. and Gerlach, L. (2005) *Improving the Emotional Health and Well-being of Young People in Secure Care: Training for Staff in Local Authority Secure Children's Homes.* London: National Children's Bureau.

Bolton, G. (2001) *Reflective Practice: Writing and Professional Development.* London: Paul Chapman Publishing.

Bonanno, G. (2009) *The Other Side of Sadness: What the New Science of Bereavement Tells Us About Life After Loss.* New York: Basic Books.

Bowlby, J. (1969) *Attachment and Loss: Vol. 1: Attachment.* New York: Basic Books.

Bowlby, J. (1980) *Maternal Deprivation; Grief in Children; Bereavement in Children; Attachment Behavior in Children; Separation Anxiety in Children.* New York: Basic Books.

Bowlby, R. (2007) 'Babies and toddlers in non-parental day-care can avoid stress and anxiety if they develop a lasting secondary attachment bond with one carer who is consistently accessible to them', *Attachment and Human Development,* 9(4), 307–319.

Bridges, W. (1991) *Managing Transition.* Reading, MA: Addison-Wesley.

Bridges, W. (2004) *Transitions: Making Sense of Life's Changes.* Cambridge, MA: Da Capo Press.

Briody, J. and McGarry, K. (2005) Using social stories to ease children's transitions, *Beyond the Journal: Young Children on the Web.* www.journal.naeyc.org/btj/200509/BriodyBTJ905.pdf (accessed 8 May 2009).

Brocklehurst, N. (2004) Is health visiting 'fully engaged' in its own future well-being?, *Community Practitioner,* June, 77(6), 214–218.

Bronfenbrenner, U. (1986). Ecology of the family as a context for human development: research perspectives, *Developmental Psychology,* 22(6), 723–742.

Brooker, L. (2008) *Supporting Transitions in the Early Years.* Maidenhead: Open University Press/McGraw Hill.

Brookfield, S. (1990) Using critical incidents to explore learners' assumptions, in J. Mezirow (ed.), *Fostering Critical Reflection in Adulthood.* San Francisco: Jossey Bass, pp. 177–193.

Broström, S. (2002) Communication and continuity in the transition from kindergarten to school, in H. Fabian and A.-W. Dunlop (eds), *Transitions in the Early Years.* London: RoutledgeFalmer, pp. 52–63.

Carpenter, B. (with J. Egerton) (2007) Family structures (as part of early support distance learning materials). www.dcsf.gov.uk/everychildmatters/healthandwell-being/ahdc/earlysupport/training/partnershiptraining/partnershiptraining/ (accessed 21 March 2012).

Childhood Bereavement Network (2010) Facts and figures. www.childhoodbereavementnetwork.org.uk/haad_about_bereavement_childhood_ff.htm (accessed 30 March 2010).

Christ, G. (2000) *Healing Children's Grief: Surviving a Parent's Death from Cancer.* New York: Oxford University Press.

Cleaver, H., Unell, I. and Aldgate, J. (2010) *Children's Needs – Parenting Capacity. The Impact of Parental Mental Illness, Problem Alcohol and Drug Use, and Domestic Violence on Children's Development.* London: HMSO, DoH.

Cooperrider, D.L. and Srivastva, S. (1987) Appreciative inquiry in organisational life, *Research in Organisational Change and Development,* 1, 129–169.

Cooperrider, D.L., Whitney, D. and Stavros, J.M. (2003) *Appreciative Inquiry Handbook.* Bedford Heights, OH: Lakeshore Publishers.

Corrigan, J. (2009) Why Study support works – lessons for education in the 21st century, presentation at QiSS Super Regional Event, Institute of Education, London University, 20 October.

Cousins, L. (2007) Making transitions easier, *Primary Headship*. www.teaching expertise.com/articles/making-transitionseasier-2994 (accessed 7 June 2010).

Covey, S.R. (2004) *The 7 Habits of Highly Effective People: Powerful Lessons in Personal Change*. London: Simon & Schuster.

Cowan, C. and Cowan, P. (2000) *When Partners Become Parents: The Big Life Change for Couples*. New York: Basic Books.

CWDC (Children's Workforce Development Council) (2010) *The Common Core of Skills and Understanding: At the Heart of What You Do*. Leeds: DCSF.

CWDC (Children's Workforce Development Council) Common Assessment Form (CAF). www.cwdcouncil.org.uk/caf (3 March 2010).

www.cwdcouncil.org.uk [10-01-2012] website no longer active all relative content can be found at http://www.education.gov.uk/search/results?q=CAF+framework

Dale, N. (1996) *Working with Families of Children with Special Needs: Partnership and Practice*. London: Routledge.

Davies, B. and Brighouse, T. (2010) Passionate leadership, *Management in Education*, 24(1), 4–6.

Davies, H. and Kinloch, H. (2000) Critical incident analysis, in V. Cree and C. Macauley (eds), *Transfer of Learning in Professional and Vocational Education*. London: Routledge.

D'Cruz, H. and Stagnitti, K. (2010) When parents love and don't love their children: some children's stories, *Child and Family Social Work*, 15, 216–225.

DCSF (Department of Children, Schools and Families) (2007) *The Early Years Foundation Stage*. London: DCSF.

DCSF (Department of Children, Schools and Families) (2009) *Progress Matters*. London: DCSF.

DCSF (Department of Children, Schools and Families) (2010) *Working Together to Safeguard Children: A Guide to Inter-agency Working to Safeguard and Promote the Welfare of Children*. Nottingham: HM Government. http://publications.dcsf. gov.uk/eOrderingDownload/00305-2010DOM-EN.PDF (accessed 7 June 2010).

DfE (Department for Education) (2001) *Special Educational Needs: Code of Practice*, London: DfE. www.direct.gov.uk/en/N11/Newsroom/DG_195045 (accessed 28 March 2012).

DfE (Department for Education) (2012) Action plan sets out radical overhaul of adoption system. London: DfE. www.education.gov.uk/inthenews/Inthenews/ a00205135/action-plan-sets-out-radical-overhaul-of-adoption-system (accessed March 2012).

DfE (Department for Education) (2012) Children looked after by local authorities in England. Cheshire: DfE. www.education.gov.uk/rsgateway/DB/SFR/s001026/ index.shtml (accessed 20 September 2012).

DfE (Department for Education) (2012) *Local transition support*. London: DfE. www.education.gov.uk/childrenandyoungpeople/sen/ahdc/a0067510/local-transition-support (accessed 13 April 2012).

DfE (Department for Education) (2012) The Early Years Foundation Stage Statutory Framework (EYFS) DfE Publications ref: 00023–2012.

DfES (Department for Education and Skills) (2001) Special Educational Needs Code of Practice. Nottingham: DfES publications ref DfES/581/2001.

DfES (Department for Education and Skills) (2003) *Every Child Matters*. London: HMSO.

DfES (Department for Education and Skills) (2005) *Extended Schools: Access to Opportunities and Services for All. A Prospectus*. Nottingham: DfES Publications ref: 1408–2005DOC-EN.

DfES (Department for Education and Skills) (2006a) *Primary National Strategy: Seamless Transitions Supporting Continuity in Young Children's Learning*. York: DfES Publications ref: 0267–2006DCL-EN.

DfES (Department for Education and Skills) (2006b) *Sure Start Children's Centre Practice Guidance*. London: The Stationery Office.

Dingwall, R. and Eekelaar, J. (1988) Families and the state: an historical perspective on the public regulation of private conduct, *Law and Policy*, 10(4), 341–361.

Dockett, S. and Perry, B. (2005) You need to know how to play safe: children's experiences of starting school, *Contemporary Issues in Early Childhood*, 6(1), 4–18.

DoH (Department of Health) (2000) *Framework for Assessment of Children in Need and their Families*. London: The Stationery Office.

DoH (Department of Health) (2004) *National Service Framework (NSF) for Children, Young People and Maternity Services*. http://publications.dcsf.gov.uk/eOrderingDownload/RW79.pdf (accessed 21 May 2010).

DoH (Department of Health) (2007) *Facing the Future: a Review of the Role of Health Visitors*. London: HMSO.

DoH (Department of Health) (2009a) *Getting It Right for Children and Families, Maximising the Contribution of the Health Visiting Team: Ambition, Action, Achievement*. London: COI.

DoH (Department of Health) (2009b) *Healthy Child Programme: Pregnancy and the First Five Years of Life*. London: HMSO.

DoH (Department of Health) (2011) *Health visitor implementation plan 2011–15: a call to action*. London: HMSO.

Dowling, M. (1995) *Starting School at Four: A Joint Endeavour*. London: Paul Chapman Publishing.

Dunlop, A. and Fabian, H. (eds) (2002) *Transitions in the Early Years: Debating Continuity and Progression for Young Children in Early Education*. London: RoutledgeFalmer.

Dunlop, A. and Fabian, H. (eds) (2007) *Informing Transitions in the Early Years: Research, Policy and Practice*. Maidenhead: Open University Press.

Dunn, M.E., Burbine, T., Bowers, C.A. and Tantleff-Dunn, S. (2001) Moderators of stress in parents of children with autism, *Community Mental Health Journal*, 37(1), 39–52.

Eaude, T. (2008) *Children's Spiritual, Moral, Social and Cultural Development*, 2nd edn. Exeter: Learning Matters.

Ecclestone, K. (2007) Lost and found in transition: the implications of identity, agency and structure for educational goals and practices, keynote presentation to Researching Transitions in Lifelong Learning Conference, 22–24 June.

Ecclestone, K., Blackmore, T., Biesta, G., Colley, H. and Hughes, M. (2005) Transitions through the lifecourse: political, professional and academic perspectives, paper presented at the Annual TLRP/ESRC Conference, University of Warwick, October 2005.

Edelman, R. (2005) *The Truth about Money*, 3rd edn. New York: HarperCollins.

Edwards, C., Gandini, L. and Forman, G. (1998) *The Hundred Languages of Children: The Reggio Emilio Approach – Advanced Reflections*, 2nd edn. Westport, CT: Ablex Publications.

Elfer, P., Goldschmeid, E. and Selleck, D. (2001) *Key Persons in Nurseries*. London: National Early Years Network.

Epstein, J. (1982) Parents' reactions to teacher practices of parent involvement, *Elementary School Journal*, 86(3), 277–294.

Fabian, H. (1998) Induction to school and transitions through Key Stage 1: practice and perceptions, University College Worcester: unpublished PhD thesis.

Fabian, H. (2000) Empowering children for transitions, paper presented at 10th European Conference on Quality of Early Childhood Education, London, 29 August–1 September.

Fabian, H. (2002) *Children Starting School: A Guide to Successful Transitions and Transfers for Teachers and Assistants*. London: David Fulton.

Fabian, H. and Dunlop, A.-W. (2006) Bridging research, policy and practice, in H. Fabian and A.-W. Dunlop (eds), *Informing Transitions in the Early Years: Research, Policy and Practice*. Maidenhead: Open University Press.

Field, F. (2010) *The Foundation Years, 1*. London: H.M. Government.

Field, J., Gallacher, J. and Ingram, R. (2009) *Researching Transitions in Lifelong Learning*. Abingdon: Routledge.

Finch, S., Dale, A. and Jackson, N. (2009) *A Review of the children's centre Outreach Workforce* CWDC/ 4 Children.

Fitzgerald, D. and Kay, J. (2008) *Working Together in Children's Services*. Abingdon: Routledge.

Foley, P. and Rixon, A. (eds) (2008) *Changing Children's Services: Working and Learning Together*. Bristol: The Open University.

Folkman, S. and Lazarus, R. (1988) The relationship between coping and emotion: implications for theory and research, *Social Science and Medicine*, 26(3), 309–317.

Fortier, L.M. and Wanlass, R.L. (1984) Family crisis following the diagnosis of a handicapped child, *Family Relations*, 33, 13–24.

Foucault, M. (1979) *Discipline and Punish: The Birth of the Prison*. London: Allen Lane.

Gerhardt, S. (2004) *Why Love Matters: How Affection Shapes a Baby's Brain*. New York: Brunner-Routledge.

Gilligan, R. (2010) Promoting positive outcomes for children in need – the importance of protective capacity in the child and their social network, in J. Horwarth (ed.), *The Child's World: The Comprehensive Guide to Assessing Children in Need*, 2nd edn. London: Jessica Kingsley Publishers, pp. 174–183.

Goldschmeid, E. and Jackson, S. (2004) *People Under Three: Young Children in Daycare*. London: Routledge.

Gray, D.E. (2003) Gender and coping: the parents of children with high functioning autism, *Social Science and Medicine*, 56(3), 631–642.

Gray, D.E. and Holden, W.J. (1992) Psycho-social well-being among the parents of children with autism, *Journal of Intellectual and Developmental Disability*, 18(2), 83–93.

Hall, D. and Elliman, D. (eds) (2003) *Health for All Children*, 4th edn. Oxford: Oxford University Press.

Hardy, B. (1968) Toward a poetics of fiction, *Novel*, 2, 5–14.

Harper, C., Marcus, R. and Moore, K. (2003) Enduring poverty and the conditions of childhood: lifecourse and intergenerational poverty transmissions, *World Development*, 31(3), 535–554.

Hastings, R.P. and Brown, T. (2002) Behaviour problems of children with autism, parental self-efficacy, and mental health, *American Journal of Mental Retardation*, 107(3), 222–232.

Hatter, B. (1996) Children and the death of a parent or grandparent, in C.A. Corr and D.M. Corr (eds), *Handbook of Childhood: Death and Bereavement*. New York: Springer Publishing.

Haynes, N. and Orrell, S. (1993) *Maslow in Psychology: An Introduction*. London: Longman.

HCC (2003) Opportunity Classes: a guide to services. Hertfordshire: HCC. www.hertsdirect.org/infobase/docs/pdfstore/opclassguide04.pdf (accessed 21 March 2012).

HCC (2010) Hertfordshire Early Years Participation Toolkit. Hertfordshire: HCC.

Heywood, J. (2009) Nothing about us without us: involving families in early support, *Community Practitioner*, 82(6), 26–29.

Hetherington, E.M., Bridges, M. and Isabella, G.M. (1998). What matters? What does not? Five perspectives on the association between marital transition and children's adjustment, *American Psychologist*, 53, 167–184.

Hinde, R.A. and Stevenson-Hinde, J. (1991) Perspectives on attachment, in C.M. Parkes, J. Stevenson-Hinde and P. Marris (eds), *Attachment Across the Life Cycle*. London: Routledge.

HM Government (2010) Information sharing. www.acm.gov.uk/informationsharing. (accessed 24 March 2010).

Hobart, C. and Frankel, J. (2003) *Childminding: A Guide to Good Practice*. Cheltenham: Nelson Thornes.

Home-Start (2011) Home-Start: Support and friendship for families. London: Home-Start. www.home-start.org.uk (accessed September 2011).

Hosking, G. and Walsh, I. (2005) *The Wave Report, Violence and What to Do about It*. Croydon: WAVE Trust.

House of Commons Health Committee (2002–3) *The Victoria Climbié Report*. Norwich: The Stationery Office.

Hyman, M. (2008) How personal constructs about 'professional identity' might act as a barrier to multi-agency working, *Educational Psychology in Practice*, 24(4), 279–288.

Illich, I. (2000) *Disabling Professions*. London: Marion Boyars Publishers.

Jarvis, J. and Trodd, L. (2008) Other ways of seeing; other ways of being: imagination as a tool for developing multi-agency professional practice for children with communication need's child language, *Teaching and Therapy*, 24(2), 211–217.

Jasper, M. and Jumaa, M. (2005) *Effective Healthcare Leadership*. Oxford: Blackwell.

Johansson, I. (2002) 'Parents' views of transition to school and their influence in this process' in H. Fabian and A.-W. Dunlop (eds), *Transitions in the Early Years: Debating Continuity and Progression for Young Children in Early Education*. London: RoutledgeFalmer.

Johnson, S., Dunn, K. and Coldron, J. (2005) *Mapping Qualifications and Training for the Children and Young People's Workforce: Common Core of Skills and Knowledge: Characteristics of Qualifications and Issues in the Field*. Sheffield: Sheffield Hallam University.

Jones, J. and Gallop, L. (2003) No time to think: protecting the reflective space in children's services, *Child Abuse Review*, 12, 1010–1016.

Kain, D.L. (2004) Owning significance: the critical incident technique in research, in K. deMarrais and S.D. Lapan (eds), *Foundations for Research: Methods of Inquiry in Education and the Social Sciences*. Mahwah, NJ: Lawrence Erlbaum Associates, pp. 69–85.

Kendrick, D., Elkan, R., Hewitt, M., Dewey, M., Blair, M., Robinson, J., Williams, D. and Brummell, K. (2000) Does home visiting improve parenting and the quality of the home environment? A systematic review and meta analysis, *Archives of Disease in Childhood*, 82, 443–451.

Kramer, L. and Houston, D (1998) Supporting families as they adopt children with special needs, *Family Relations*, 47(4), 423–432.

Kübler-Ross, E. (1969) *On Death and Dying*. New York: Macmillan.

Laevers, F., Vandenbussche, E., Kog, M. and Depondt, L. (1997) *A Process-oriented Child Monitoring System for Young Children*. Centre for Experiential Education: Katholieke Universiteit Leuven.

Lamb, B. (2009) *Inquiry into Parental Confidence in the Special Education Needs System*. London. www.dcsf.gov.uk/lambinquiry (accessed December 2009).

Laming, Lord (2009) *The Protection of Children in England: A Progress Report*. London: HMSO.

Larson, C. (1980) Efficacy of prenatal and postpartum home visits on child health and development, *Pediatrics*, 66, 191–197.

Leadbetter, J. (2006) New ways of working and new ways of being: multi-agency working and professional identity, *Educational and Child Psychology*, 23(4), 47–58.

Lee, V. and Burkham, D. (2002) Inequality at the starting gate, www.epi.org/content.cfm?id=617 (1 of 4) (accessed 10 May 2010).

Leeds Animation Workshop (2005) *Not Too Young To Grieve* (DVD/VHS). Leeds: Leeds Animation Workshop.

Leeds Multi-agency Transition Strategy 2010–2015 (2012) *A person-centred approach to transition between services for children and services for adults*. Leeds: Leeds City Council Communications.

Luther, E.H. (2005) Coping and social support for parents of children with autism, *Journal of School Nursing*, 21(1), 40–47.

Lynch, E. and Hanson, M. (1992) *Developing Cross-Cultural Competence: A Guide for Working with Young Children and Their Families*. Baltimore, MD: Paul H. Brookes Publishing Company.

Marshall, J. (1994) Revisioning organizations by developing female values, in R. Boot, J. Lawrence and J. Morris (eds), *Managing the Unknown by Creating New Futures*. London: McGraw Hill, pp 165–183.

Martin, V. (2003) *Leading Change in Health and Social Care*. London: Routledge.

Marvin, R.S. and Pianta, R.C. (1996) Mothers' reactions to their child's diagnosis: reasons with security of attachment, *Journal of Clinical Child Psychology*, 25, 436–445.

Maslow, A.H. (1943) A theory of human motivation, *Psychological Review*, 50(4), 370–396.

McKee, T.E., Harvey, E., Danforth, J.S., Ulaszek, W.R. and Friedman, J.L. (2004) The relation between parental coping styles and parent-child interactions before and after treatment for children with ADHD and oppositional behaviour, *Journal of Clinical Child and Adolescent Psychology*, 33(1), 158–168.

McKellar, L., Pincombe, J. and Henderson, A. (2009) Coming ready or not! Preparing parents for parenthood, *British Journal of Midwifery*, 17(3), 160–167.

McLeod, A. (2008) *Listening to Children: A Practitioner's Guide*. London: Jessica Kinglsey Publishers.

Midence, K. and O'Neill, M. (1999) The experience of parents in the diagnosis of autism: a pilot study, *Autism*, 3(3), 273–285.

Milbourne, L., Macrae, S. and Maguire, M. (2003) Collaborative solutions or new policy problems: exploring multi-agency partnership in education and health care, *Education Policy and Politics*, 18(1), 19–35.

Mintzberg, H. (1998) Covert leadership: notes on managing professionals, *Harvard Business Review*, November–December, 140–147.

Molyneux, J. (2001) Interprofessional teamworking: what makes teams work well?, *Journal of Interprofessional Care*, 15(1), 29–35.

Montes, G. and Halterman, J.S. (2007) Psychological functioning and coping among mothers of children with autism: a population-based study, *Pediatrics*, 119(5), 1040–1046.

Morrow, G., Malin, N. and Jennings, T. (2005) Interprofessional teamworking for child and family referral in a sure start local programme, *Journal of Interprofessional Care*, 19(2), 93–101.

Mortimer, H. (2004) Hearing children's voices in the early years, *British Journal of Learning Support*, 19(4), 169–174.

Moss, P. (2008) Foreword, in A. Paige-Smith and A. Craft (eds), *Developing Reflective Practice in the Early Years*. London: Open University Press.

Munro, E. (2011) *The Munro Review of Child Protection: Final Report, A Child-centred System*. London: Crown.

National Children's Bureau (2009) Bereaved children more likely to have faced other difficult events in childhood. Media release. www.ncb.org.uk/default.aspx?page=2173 (accessed 10 March 2010).

National Society for the Prevention of Cruelty to Children (2009) *Emotional Abuse.* www.nspcc.org.uk/helpandadvice/whatchidabuse/emotional/Abuse (accessed 23 April 2010).

Neil-Hall, J. (2007) Attachment: supporting young children's emotional well-being – early years update. www.teachingexpertise.com (accessed 20 February 2010).

Newman, T. and Blackburn, S. (2002) *Transitions in the Lives of Children and Young People: Resilience Factors.* Barnardo's Policy, Research and Influencing Unit, for Interchange.

NICE (National Institute for Health and Clinical Excellence) (2011) Autism: recognition, referral and diagnosis of children and young people on the autism spectrum. http://guidance.nice.org.uk/nicemedia/live/13572/56424/56424.pdf (accessed 28 September 2011).

NMC (Nursing and Midwifery Council) (2008) The code: standards of conduct, performance and ethics for nurses and midwives. www.nmck.org/aArticle. aspx?ArticleID=3056#4 (12 March 2010).

Oates, J. (2006) Ethical frameworks for research with human participants, in S. Potter (2006) *Doing Postgraduate Research*, 2nd edn. London: Sage, pp. 200–227.

O'Connor, A. (2007) *All about ... transitions. The Early Years Foundation Stage, Primary, National Strategy.* London: Crown.

O'Connor, A. (2010) Transitions, speech at a Nursery World Conference.

OECD (2006) *Early Childhood Education and Care.* Paris: OECD.

Ofsted (2004) *Transition from the Reception Year to Year 1: An Evaluation by HMI. HMI 2221.* London: Ofsted

Olds, D.L., Kitzman, H.J., Cole, R.E. et al. (2010) Enduring effects of prenatal and infancy home visiting by nurses on maternal life course and government spending – follow up of a randomized trial among children at age 12, *Archives of Pediatric and Adolescent Medicine*, 164(5), 419–424.

Page, J.M. (2000) *Reframing the Early Childhood Curriculum: Educational Imperatives for the Future.* London: RoutledgeFalmer.

Pain, H. (1999) Coping with a child with disabilities from the parents' perspective: the function of information, *Child: Care, Health and Development*, 25(4), 299–312.

Palaiologou, I. (2009) *Childhood Observation*, 3rd edn. Exeter: Learning Matters.

Palmer, S. (2006) *Toxic Childhood.* London: Orion.

Parton, N. (2000) Some thoughts on the relationship between theory and practice in and for social work, *British Journal of Social Work*, 30, 449–483.

Pedro-Carroll, J. (2005) Fostering children's resilience in the aftermath of divorce, *Family Court Review*, 43, 52–64.

Piaget, Jean (1997) *The Development of Thought: Equilibriation of Cognitive Structures.* New York: Viking Press.

Pianta, R., Steinburg, M. and Rollins, B. (1995) The first two years of school: teacher–child relationships and deflections in children's classroom adjustment, *Development and Psychopathology*, 7(2), 295–312.

Pre-school Learning Alliance (2009) *The New Child in Focus.* London: PLA.

Pugh, G. and Duffy, P. (2006) *Contemporary Issues in Early Years.* London: Sage.

Quinn Patton, M. (2002) *Qualitative Research and Evaluation Methods*, 3rd edn. Thousand Oaks, CA: Sage.

Recnews.co.uk. Working mums count long-term impact of recession. www.recnews. co.uk/index.php/2010/02/10/working-mums-count-long-term-impact-of-recession/ (accessed 16 May 2010).

Regan, P. and Ireland, L. (2009) In the moment, *Community Practitioner*, 82(5), 34–35.

Rehal, F. (2008) Ideology of integrated working, *Community Practitioner*, 81(2), 42–43.

Ricciardi, C.R. (2004) President's message: Appreciative Inquiry: promoting individual and organisational change, *Journal of Pediatric Health Care*, 18(6), A16.

Rich, A. and Parker, D.L. (1995) Reflection and critical incident analysis: ethical and moral implications of their use within nursing and midwifery education, *Journal of Advanced Nursing*, 22(6), 1050–1057.

Rivers, J.W. and Stoneman, Z. (2003) Sibling relationships when a child has autism: marital stress and support coping, *Journal of Autism and Developmental Disorders*, 33(4), 383–394.

Roberts, R. (2006) *Self-esteem and Early Learning*, 2nd edn. London: Paul Chapman.

Robins, A. and Callan, S. (eds) (2009) *Managing Early Years Settings: Supporting and Leading Teams*. London: Sage.

Robinson, M. (2008) *Child Development from Birth to Eight: a Journey through the Early Years*. Maidenhead: Open University Press.

Robinson, M. (2009) Separate ways, *Nursery World*, 10 December, 22–23.

Rushmer, R. and Pallis, G. (2002) Interprofessional working: the wisdom of integrated working and the disaster of blurred boundaries, *Public Money & Management*, October–December, 23(1), 59–66.

Sanders, D., White, G., Burge, B., Sharp, C., Eames, A., McEune, R. and Grayson, H. (2005) *A Study of the Transition from the Foundation Stage to Key Stage 1 Research Report*, April. Nottingham: National Foundation for Educational Research (NfER).

Schön, D. (1987) *Educating the Reflective Practitioner*. San Francisco: Jossey-Bass.

Shear, M. (2009) Grief and depression: treatments decisions for bereaved children and adults, *American Journal of Psychiatry*,166, 746–748.

Shields, P. (2009) School doesn't feel as much of a partnership: parents' perceptions of their children's transitions from nursery school to reception class, *Early Years*, 29(3), 237–248.

Silverman, P. (2000) *Never Too Young to Know: Death in Children's Lives*. New York: Oxford University Press, pp. 93–123.

Sinclair, A. (2007) *0–5: How Small Children Make a Big Difference*. London: The Work Foundation.

Siraj-Blatchford, I., Clarke, K. and Needham, M. (2007) *The Team around the Child: Multi-agency Working in the Early Years*, Stoke-on-Trent and Sterling, PA: Trentham Books.

Sloper, P., Beecham, J., Clarke, S., Franklin, A., Moran, N. and Cousworth, L. (2010) *Models of Multi-Agency services for Transition to Adult Services for Disabled Young People and those with Complex Health Needs: Impact and Cost*. York: SPRU.

Smith, N. (2003) Transition from nursery to school playground: an intervention programme to promote emotional and social development, paper presented at the 13th European Early Childhood Education Research Association (EECERA) Conference, University of Strathclyde, Glasgow, 3–6 September.

Smith, P.K., Cowie, H. and Blades, M. (1998) *Understanding Children's Development*. Malden, MA: Blackwell Publishers.

Sunderland, M. (2006) *What Every Parent Needs to Know*. London: Dorling Kindersley.

Sure Start (2002) *Supporting Families Who Have Children with Special Needs and Disabilities*. London: DFES.

Teaching Agency (2012) Review of the Early Years Professional Status Standards, May 2012. http://markallen-cms.co.uk/digital_assets/eyps_standards_2012.pdf (accessed 16 July 2012).

TCRU (Thomas Coram Research Unit) (2006) Models of good practice in joined-up assessment: working for children with 'significant and complex needs'. http://

publications.dcsf.gov.uk/default.aspx?PageFunction=productdetails&Page Mode=publications&ProductId=RW79& (accessed 21 May 2010).

Thurtle, V. (2007) All for one, one for all, *Community Practitioner*, 80(12), 44–45.

Training and Development Agency (TDA) (2009) *What Are Extended Services?* Manchester: TDA.

Tritschler, E. and Yarwood, J. (2007) Relating to families through their seasons of life, *Kai Tiaiki Nursing New Zealand*, 13(5), 18–20.

Trodd, L. and Chivers, L. (2011) *Interprofessional Working in Practice: Learning and Working Together for Children and Families*. Maidenhead: Open University Press

Twoy, R., Connolly, P.M. and Novak, J.M. (2007) Coping strategies used by parents of children with autism, *Journal of the American Academy of Nurse Practitioners*, 19(5), 251–260.

Turnbull, A. (2006) Children's Transitions: A Literature Review. Cambridgeshire Children'sFund.http://www.cambridgeshire.gov.uk/NR/rdonlyres/0F47EDD3-B534-4319-9F8C-70870DCF42E4/0/CHILDRESTRANSITIONS.pdf

Turnell, A. (2010) *The Signs of Safety: A Comprehensive Briefing Paper*. Available at: www.scie-socialcareonline.org.uk/profile.asp? guid=78c4826a-8b52-4b6d-bd7a-5ec28f98ec6e (accessed 7 November 2011).

UN General Assembly (20 November 1989) *Convention on the Rights of the Child*, United Nations, Treaty Series, vol. 1577, p. 3. www.unhcr.org/refworld/docid/3ae6b38f0.html (accessed 19 March 2012).

UNICEF (2009) *The State of the World's Children: Executive Summary*. New York: United Nations Children's Fund. www.unicef.org/publications/index_51777.html (accessed 7 June 2010).

Usher, R., Bryant, I. and Johnston, R. (1997) *Adult Education and the Postmodern Challenge: Learning Beyond the Limits*. London: Routledge.

Varley, S. (1992) *Badger's Parting Gifts*. London. Collins Picture Lions.

Vogler, P., Crivello, G. and Woodhead, M. (2008) *Early Childhood Transitions Research: A Review of Concepts, Theory and Practice*, BvLF Working Papers in Early Childhood Development 48, The Hague, The Netherlands: Bernard van Leer Foundation.

Wall, K. (2011) *Special Needs and Early Years*. London: Sage.

Way, P. (2010) Co-creating memory: supporting very young children, in B. Monroe and F. Kraus (eds), *Brief Interventions with Bereaved Children*. Oxford: Oxford University Press.

Wenger, E. (1998) *Communities of Practice: Learning Meaning and Identity*. Cambridge: Cambridge University Press.

Winston's Wish (2010) Facts and figures. www.winstonswish.org.uk/page.asp? section=0001000100040005 (20 April 20 2010).

Wolfenstein, M. (1966) How is mourning possible?, *Psychoanalytic Study of the Child*, 21, 93–123.

Woodhead, M. and Brooker, L. (2008) A sense of belonging, *Early Childhood Matters*, 111, 3–6.

Woodhead, M. and Moss, P. (2007) *Early Childhood and Primary Education. Early Childhood in Focus 2: Transitions in the Lives of Young Children*. Milton Keynes: Open University Press.

Yagla Mack, K. (2001) Childhood family disruptions and adult well-being: the differential effects of divorce and parental death, *Death Studies*, 25(5), 419–443.

Young Minds (2012) *Young Minds in Schools*. www.youngminds.org.uk/training_services/young_minds_in_schools/wellbeing/transitions (accessed 20 October 2012).

Index